Barrier Lake—

Emerald Lake Lodge—Yoho National Park

Howse Peak, Mistaya Valley—Banff National Park

Jasper Townsite, Mount Edith Cavell—Jasper National Park

Lake Louise—Banff National Park

Maligne Lake—Jasper National Park

Moon over Mount Rundle – Banff National Park

Moraine Lake, Banff National Park

Mount Robson—Mount Robson Provincial Park

Mount Athabasca, Sunwapta River—Jasper National Park

Prince of Wales Hotel—Waterton Lakes National Park

Rocky Mountaineer Touring Train—East of Canmore,
Bow River Valley, Mount Lougheed

Sunset over Castle Mountain—Banff National Park

Takakkaw Falls—Yoho National Park

Vermilion Pass—Banff National Park

Winter Moonrise over Vermilion Lakes—Banff National Park

A Taste of the
Canadian Rockies
Cookbook

MYRIAM LEIGHTON AND CHIP OLVER

TouchWood
Editions

VICTORIA | VANCOUVER | CALGARY

TouchWood Editions

108 – 17665 66A Avenue	PO Box 468
Surrey, BC V3S 2A7	Custer, WA
www.touchwoodeditions.com	98240-0468

LIBRARY AND ARCHIVES CANADA CATALOGUING IN PUBLICATION

Leighton, Myriam, 1962–
    A taste of the Canadian Rockies / Myriam Leighton and Chip Olver.
Includes index.
ISBN 978-1-894898-84-3
    1. Cookery—Rocky Mountains, Canadian (B.C. and Alta.). 2. Cookery,
Canadian—Alberta style. I. Olver, Chip, 1955- II. Title.
TX715.6.L458 2008   641.597123'3   C2008-906358-9

LIBRARY OF CONGRESS CONTROL NUMBER: 2008905356

Proofread: Marial Shea
Interior design: Jacqui Thomas
Cover images: Douglas Leighton
Interior colour images: Douglas Leighton

Printed in Canada

TouchWood Editions acknowledges the financial support for its publishing program from
the Government of Canada through the Book Publishing Industry Development Program
(BPIDP), Canada Council for the Arts, and the province of British Columbia through the
British Columbia Arts Council and the Book Publishing Tax Credit.

This book has been produced on 100% post-consumer recycled paper, processed chlorine
free and printed with vegetable-based dyes.

Contents

Banff Avenue and Cascade Mountain, *1887*

Introduction *and* Acknowledgments

A Taste of the Canadian Rockies includes mouth-watering recipes from restaurants in the towns of Banff, Jasper, Lake Louise, Waterton and Canmore as well as selections from the resorts and backcountry lodges that are nestled throughout the Canadian Rockies. Some distinguishing characteristics of tourist destinations are the incredible variety of dining opportunities, the outstanding quality offered in the restaurants and the chefs who come from around the world to create dishes to tempt you and your friends. Although some of our featured restaurants and chefs are now gone, the recipes shared here remain favourites.

You can imagine how difficult it was to select the eating establishments and recipes that are represented in this collection. (At last count the town of Banff alone had more than 70 restaurant listings in the phone book.) We started with our own favourites, asked others what their favourites were and then combined the lists.

The original version of this Canadian best seller was published in 1985 as *A Taste of Banff.* We realized your visit to the Canadian Rockies includes other locations you'd like memories of and so expanded the book to give you just that.

Warm thanks to:

- Douglas Leighton, for the original book idea, for the spectacular colour photographs throughout the book and for his support.

- Jim, Jamie, Linda and Thomas Olver with love for their support.

- The chefs and restaurant owners who made this book possible and who supplied their favourite recipes for you to recreate at home.

We are delighted to present this book for your enjoyment. Now that it is done we are anxious to get into our own kitchens to try out more of these wonderful dishes and impress family and friends!

Cheers and happy dining,
Myriam Leighton and Chip Olver

Baker with display board, *1925*

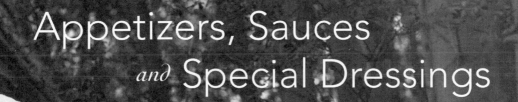

Appetizers, Sauces
and Special Dressings

Spinach *and* Cambozola Cheese Wrapped *in* Phyllo *with* Fresh Fruit Salsa

Lara Christie, *Executive Chef*
DEER LODGE, LAKE LOUISE

Serves 4

Large white onion, sliced thin	1
Unsalted butter	2 tbsp (30 ml)
Fresh spinach, washed	8 oz (250 g)
Salt	to taste
Ground white pepper	to taste
Curry powder	pinch
Cambozola cheese	8 oz (250 g)
Phyllo dough	4 sheets
Melted butter	as needed

Sweat the onion in a saucepan with the butter. When onion is translucent add washed spinach, salt, pepper and curry powder. Cook spinach completely until vibrant green. Cut Cambozola into 4 even slices.

Note: The next few steps need to be done quickly so go over method beforehand. Preheat the oven to 375°F (190°C). Take each sheet of phyllo dough and lay out on the counter. Brush two of the sheets completely with melted butter, cover each of these sheets with the remaining dough to make a second layer. Brush second layer very lightly with more melted butter.

Cut the two buttered phyllo pieces in half widthwise so there are 4 equal pieces left. Divide cooked spinach into 4 portions. Place each spinach portion at the end of each phyllo piece, place each piece of cheese onto the spinach.

Fold side edges of phyllo up onto the cheese and spinach. (This is so the cheese doesn't ooze out when cooking.) Brush the folded edges with melted butter and proceed to roll up the cheese and spinach in the dough very loosely.

Place cheese bundles onto a baking tray with the seam side down so dough doesn't unwrap when baked. Bake for 5 to 7 minutes, until golden brown. Spoon fresh fruit salsa (recipe follows) over each one and serve piping hot.

FRESH FRUIT SALSA

Strawberries	2–3
Honeydew melon	½
Cantaloupe melon	½
Kiwi fruit	1
Fresh pineapple	¼
Mango or papaya	1
Cilantro, chopped	2 tbsp (30 ml)
Mint, chopped	2 tbsp (30 ml)

Dice all of the fruit into ¼-inch (5-mm) pieces and mix in a bowl. Add chopped cilantro and mint. *Option:* You can add some zip to this salsa, just add some diced jalapeño pepper. Set salsa aside. Salsa can be made a day ahead if needed.

We are entering the defiles of the Rocky Mountains by the Athabaska River, the woods of Pine are stunted, full of Branches to the ground, and the Aspin, Willow, not much better; strange to say, there is a strong belief that the haunt of the Mammoth, is about this defile, I questioned several, none could positively say, they had seen him, but their belief I found firm and not to be shaken.

David Thompson, *explorer*
JANUARY 5TH, 1811, FROM *JASPER NATIONAL PARK* BY M.B. WILLIAMS, 1928

Smoked Trout Crostini

Milos Moravcik, *Executive Chef*
INNS OF BANFF PARK, BANFF

Serves 4

Smoked trout fillets (skinless, boneless)	½ lb (250 g)
Plain yogurt	½ cup (125 ml)
Mayonnaise	¼ cup (50 ml)
Fresh lemon juice	1 tsp (5 ml)
Fresh dill, chopped very fine	1 tbsp (15 ml)
Onion, minced	2 tbsp (30 ml)
Freshly ground black pepper	to taste
Salt	to taste

Place all ingredients in a food processor and purée until you reach a smooth consistency. Cover mixture and refrigerate for 3 to 4 hours.

CROSTINI

French baguette bread	1
Fresh basil, minced	2 tbsp (30 ml)
Unsalted butter, melted	¼ cup (50 ml)
Garlic, minced	1 tbsp (15 ml)
Parsley, chopped	1 tbsp (15 ml)

Preheat oven to 300°F (150°C). Cut baguette into ½-inch (1-cm) slices diagonally and place on baking sheet. In a bowl mix the basil, melted butter, garlic and chopped parsley. Brush both sides of the bread slices with the mixture. Bake, occasionally turning over the crostini, until they become toasted golden brown. Set aside to cool. Spread each crostini with the smoked trout mixture, garnish with a sprig of fresh dill and serve.

Garlic Herb Soufflé

Scott Schroeder, *Executive Chef*
LAKE O'HARA LODGE, YOHO NATIONAL PARK

Serves 6

Garlic cloves, peeled, finely chopped	6
Onion, finely chopped	2 tbsp (30 ml)
Olive oil	as needed
Thick béchamel sauce	1½ cups (375 ml)
Mixed fresh herbs, finely chopped	3 tbsp (45 ml)
Salt and pepper	to taste
Eggs, separated	4
Butter and flour	to coat baking dishes

Butter and flour 6 individual soufflé dishes. Preheat oven to 400°F (200°C).

Lightly sauté garlic and onion in olive oil—do not brown. In a medium-sized mixing bowl, mix together béchamel sauce, sautéed garlic and onion, fresh herbs, salt and pepper. Add egg yolks and mix well. Whisk egg whites until stiff. Fold into egg yolk mixture. Fill soufflé dishes and bake immediately for 20 minutes or until puffed and firm in the middle.

Serve immediately.

—*"What is life?" asked the wise looking man in spectacles. "Two weeks in Banff," said the Calgary girl, "that's life for me."*

BANFF CRAG AND CANYON, AUGUST 20, 1904

Quesadilla *with* Hot Italian Sausage *and* Avocado Salsa

Milos Moravcik, *Executive Chef*
INNS OF BANFF PARK, BANFF

Serves 4

Hot Italian sausage	½ lb (250 g)
Flour tortillas	4
Monterey Jack cheese, shredded	2 cups (500 ml)
Mild cheddar cheese, shredded	1 cup (250 ml)
Italian sun-dried tomatoes in olive oil	½ cup (125 ml)
Jalapeño peppers, chopped fine	2 tbsp (30 ml)
Chives, chopped fine	½ cup (125 ml)

Remove Italian sausage from casing and fry in a skillet until cooked. Set aside.

Preheat oven to 375°F (190°C). Lay the tortillas flat on a cookie sheet and distribute the cheese equally among them making sure to cover the entire areas except for a ¼-inch (5-mm) border. Remove sun-dried tomatoes from olive oil, pat dry and chop fine. Distribute the Italian sausage, sun-dried tomatoes, jalapeño and chives equally over the tortillas.

Place cookie sheet in the oven and bake just until the cheese has melted, approximately 8 to 10 minutes. Remove from the oven and fold over each quesadilla, cut into 4 pieces and serve with Avocado Salsa and a dollop of sour cream.

AVOCADO SALSA

Avocados, peeled, seeded, diced	2
Tomatoes, seeded and diced	½ cup (125 ml)
Cilantro, chopped fine	¼ cup (50 ml)
Red onion, diced	3 tbsp (45 ml)
Garlic clove, minced	1
Fresh lime juice	1 tbsp (15 ml)

Jalapeño peppers, seeded and diced	1 tsp (5 ml)
Coarse salt	1 tsp (5 ml)
Fresh ground black pepper	⅛ tsp (1 ml)

Place all ingredients in a bowl and mix gently. Salsa tastes best on the day it is prepared.

Hot Artichoke, Cheddar *and* Crab Dip

Dave Husereau, *Chef de Cuisine*
FIDDLE RIVER SEAFOOD COMPANY, JAS-
PER

Serves 4

Artichoke hearts, drained	6-oz (170-ml) can
Mayonnaise	⅔ cup (150 ml)
Sour cream	⅔ cup (150 ml)
Parmesan cheese	⅔ cup (150 ml)
Crabmeat	¼ cup (50 ml)
Dried tarragon	1 tbsp (15 ml)
Cheddar cheese, shredded	½ cup (125 ml)

Preheat oven to 440°F (220°C). Chop artichokes and mix well with mayonnaise, sour cream, Parmesan, crabmeat and tarragon. Bake in earthenware dish topped with cheddar until bubbling. Serve with crudities such as nacho chips, carrot sticks or fennel, etc.

Buffalo Satay

Tom Hayes, *Executive Chef*
BUFFALO MOUNTAIN LODGE, BANFF

MARINADE

Hoisin sauce	1 cup (250 ml)
Plum sauce	6 tbsp (90 ml)
Rice vinegar	½ cup (125 ml)
Honey	2 tbsp (30 ml)
Dry sherry	2 tbsp (30 ml)
Chinese chili sauce	1 tbsp (15 ml)
Garlic cloves, chopped	2 to 4
Green onions, chopped	2
Coriander seed	1 tbsp (15 ml)

Mix marinade ingredients.

MEAT   Serves 4 to 6

Buffalo meat	1 lb (500 g)

Slice meat into very thin strips and ribbon on to a bamboo skewer. Marinate 24 hours or more. Grill on barbecue or cook under broiler. Serve with dipping sauce.

Variation: Can be made with beef, chicken or pork.

DIPPING SAUCE

Peanuts, chopped	¼ cup (50 ml)
Lime juice	2 tbsp (30 ml)
Green onion, minced	2
Garlic cloves, chopped	2
Coconut milk	¾ cup (175 ml)

Peanut butter	4 tbsp (60 ml)
Dark soya sauce	1 tbsp (15 ml)
Brown sugar	1 tbsp (15 ml)
Cumin	1 tsp (5 ml)
Coriander seed	1½ tsp (7 ml)
Chinese chili sauce	1 tbsp (15 ml)

Mix all ingredients together.

Delicious Cheese Rolls (Tiropeta)

Tom and Maria Lambropoulos, *Owners*
BALKAN, THE GREEK RESTAURANT, BANFF

Serves 12 to 14

Eggs, separated	6
Feta cheese, crumbled	2 cups (500 ml)
Cottage cheese	2 cups (500 ml)
Blue cheese (optional)	½ cup (125 ml)
Phyllo	2 lb (1 kg)
Butter, melted	1 lb (500 g)

Preheat oven to 350°F (180°C). Beat egg yolks, add feta cheese, mix well. Add cottage cheese and blue cheese, mix well. Beat egg whites stiff and fold them in. Cut phyllo sheets in halves or thirds, brush with hot melted butter. Place 1 teaspoon (5 ml) of cheese mixture in the bottom centre of phyllo. Fold over ⅓ on each side, brush with hot melted butter. Roll up as for jelly roll. Place on cookie sheet. Bake for 15 minutes or until done.

Cilantro Chili Mayonnaise

Kim Purdy
COYOTE'S DELI & GRILL, BANFF

Makes 3 cups

Cilantro, chopped	1 cup (250 ml)
Garlic cloves	8
Jalapeño chili peppers	2
Ground cumin	4 tsp (20 ml)
Mayonnaise	2 cups (500 ml)

In a food processor or blender, purée the cilantro, garlic, chilies and cumin.

Stir into the mayonnaise.

May be refrigerated. Great for perking up sandwiches, burgers or for a vegetable dip.

If you think this will be too spicy for your tastes you can calm it down by removing the seeds from the Jalapeño chilies.

The Canadian Pacific Railway ought to have a commission on detective cameras, kodaks, hawkeyes, etc. ... Whenever you stop at a station, all the steps for getting down are packed with people taking pot shots with kodaks. American children learn kodaking long before they learn to behave themselves ... every operator imagines he is going to kodak an Indian; but the wily Indian sits in the shade, where instantaneous photography availeth not, and, if he observes himself being 'time-exposed' covers his head with a blanket.

Douglas Sladen,
1895, IN *ON THE CARS AND OFF*

Skoki Health Bread

SKOKI LODGE, BANFF NATIONAL PARK

BREAD	Makes 4 loaves
Warm water	4½ cups (1.125 l)
Oil	½ cup (125 ml)
Honey	½ cup (125 ml)
Molasses	½ cup (125 ml)
Salt	5 tsp (25 ml)
Whole wheat flour	4 cups (1 l)
Sesame seeds	¼ cup (50 ml)
Millet	¼ cup (50 ml)
Poppy seeds	¼ cup (50 ml)
Yeast	4 tsp (20 ml)
Baker's flour	8 cups (2 l)

Combine all the ingredients in a large bowl. Add enough flour to make a kneadable ball, then knead for 10 minutes or more until dough is smooth as a baby's bottom. Let rise until doubled in bulk. Punch down, shape into loaves and let rise in the loaf pans for about 40 minutes. Bake until hollow sounding when tapped.

GLAZE (OPTIONAL)

Egg, beaten
Poppy seeds, as needed

To glaze, when dough is in pans, paint with egg before rising. Shake poppy seeds over tops.

Baked Goat Cheese Wrapped *in* Phyllo Pastry

Aaron Cundliffe, *Executive Chef*
EMERALD LAKE LODGE, YOHO NATIONAL PARK

Serves 2

Mild goat cheese	½ lb (250 g)
Phyllo pastry	1 sheet
Medium red bell pepper, roasted, diced	1
Clarified butter	½ lb (250 g)

Preheat the oven to 350°F (180°C). Cut phyllo in half, brush with clarified butter on outer edges. Place half the goat cheese on each of the phyllo sheets. Place the diced pepper over the goat cheese. Fold each of the sides over the goat cheese. Brush the finished product with clarified butter. Bake for 15 minutes or until brown. Serve with salsa.

SALSA

Medium tomato, peeled, seeded	1
Onion	½
Garlic clove, minced	to taste
Tabasco	splash
Worcestershire sauce	splash
Thyme	pinch
Basil	pinch
Oregano	pinch
Lemon juice	pinch

Combine all the salsa ingredients and allow to sit refrigerated for a couple of hours.

Ticino Marinated Salmon

Markus Wespi, *Chef/Co-owner*
TICINO RESTAURANT, BANFF

For 1 side of salmon

Side of fresh salmon	1–1½ lb (500–750 g)
Brown sugar	2 cups (500 g)
White peppercorns, crushed	¼ cup (50 ml)
Allspice, crushed	¼ cup (50 ml)
Salt or rock salt	½ cup (125 ml)
Liquid smoke	1 tbsp (15 ml)
Fresh dill, chopped	1 bunch (about 2 cups/500 ml)

Combine all ingredients except the dill, pat the mixture over the salmon (skin down). Place dill on top and marinate (covered) in the refrigerator for 3 days.

After 3 days take marinade off and strain. The liquid from marinade can be mixed with 1 tsp (5 ml) Dijon mustard and a little Pernod. Brush on slices as you serve salmon. Or marinade can be mixed with fresh dill and sour cream as a dip.

Salmon can also be served warm in portions as you heat it in the oven at 350°F (180°C) for approximately 10 minutes.

The Rocky Mountain Bighorn soon may become milady's latest pet ... the tamed sheep ... can be taught little tricks ... and not only do them for the caretaker but for any visitor. All folks look alike to sheep, once tamed.

BANFF CRAG AND CANYON, MAY 25, 1928

Broiled Shrimp *with an* Asian Sauce

Daniel Martineau, *Chef/Partner*
BAKER CREEK BISTRO, LAKE LOUISE

ASIAN SAUCE

Sunflower seeds, roasted	½ cup (125 ml)
Garlic cloves	3
Soya sauce	¼ cup (50 ml)
White vinegar	¼ cup (50 ml)
Water	¼ cup (50 ml)
Tabasco	3 drops
Worcestershire	3 drops
Sesame oil	1 tbsp (15 ml)
Olive oil	1 tbsp (15 ml)
Cayenne	pinch
Freshly ground black pepper	to taste

With a food processor, grind the sunflower seeds and garlic. Add the remaining ingredients and blend well. Refrigerate and stir well before serving.

BROILED SHRIMP   Serves 4

Shrimp	20
Bamboo skewers	4
Olive oil and lemon juice, mixed (each)	3 tbsp (45 ml)
Fresh ground black pepper	to taste
Lemon wedge or crown garnish	4
Parsley sprig	4
Sesame seeds, toasted	2 tbsp (30 ml)

Peel, devein and rinse shrimp in cold water. Pat dry with a cloth. Put 5 shrimp on each skewer and dip in olive oil/lemon mixture. Cook on a preheated broiler or barbecue—2 minutes on each side. Season with black pepper.

While the shrimp are cooking, garnish 4 plates. Place cooked skewered shrimp on the dressing. Sprinkle with sesame seeds and serve.

At the Baker Creek Bistro, we have used the Asian Sauce with smoked lamb, lobster, chicken wings and avocado salad. Surely you will discover other items to use it with.

Mr. Helm ... became hopelessly lost ... when found, he was or seemed to be, partly delirious, keeping up a strange conversation about a lot of mermaids he saw ... through a large hole in a rock ... We all know Mr. Helm is of sound mind ... (and) it was some days before ... the mystery was cleared ... eight ladies who were bathing in the Cave, complained of a nasty, bold man watching them sporting in the waters of life.

Mr. Helm was never a confirmed bachelor ... and now carries a set of opera glasses and swears that next time he will not be fooled easily.

BANFF CRAG AND CANYON, JULY 26, 1902

Baked Camembert

Claude Harvey, *Chef de Cuisine*
JOSHUA'S RESTAURANT, BANFF

	Per serving
Puff pastry	3 oz (90 g)
Camembert	2½ oz (75 g)
Egg	1

Preheat the oven to 400°F (200°C). Roll the puff pastry to a size of 4 × 4 inches (10 × 10 cm). Place the Camembert onto one half of the dough and egg wash the edges before folding over. Egg wash the outside and bake for 5 to 10 minutes, until lightly browned.

MUSTARD SAUCE	Makes about 1 cup
Butter	1 tsp (5 ml)
Garlic	½ tsp (2 ml)
Shallots	½ tsp (2 ml)
Coarse mustard	1 tsp (5 ml)
Dijon mustard	1 tsp (5 ml)
White wine	⅓ cup (75 ml)
Whipping cream	⅔ cup (150 ml)

Heat butter in a small pan. Add garlic, shallots and both mustards. Add the white wine and reduce by half. Add the cream and reduce again 2 to 3 minutes (to your liking). Pour sauce on a plate and place baked Camembert in middle. Garnish with a parsley sprig and serve.

A number of tourists made the discovery on Friday that showers in Banff contain considerable wetness.

BANFF CRAG AND CANYON, JULY 29, 1901

Mussels *with* Saffron Sauce

Claude Harvey, *Chef de Cuisine*
JOSHUA'S RESTAURANT, BANFF

	Per serving
Mussels, medium size	12–15
White wine	⅔ cup (150 ml)
Garlic, minced	2 tsp (10 ml)
Shallots	2 tsp (10 ml)

Place the mussels in a skillet and add the wine, garlic and shallots. Cover and cook on high burner for 3 to 4 minutes.

Remove the mussels from the skillet. Keep the wine and garlic to finish the sauce.

SAFFRON SAUCE

Saffron	pinch
Whipping cream	½ cup (125 ml)
Parmesan cheese	2 tbsp (30 ml)
Julienne of: celery, carrots, leeks, green and red peppers	just enough to garnish or more for a meal

To the wine and garlic mix, add saffron, cream, Parmesan cheese and julienne. Reduce to desired consistency. Add the mussels with the sauce and serve.

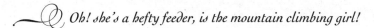 *Oh! she's a hefty feeder, is the mountain climbing girl!*

FROM ANONYMOUS POEM, "THE MOUNTAIN CLIMBING GIRL,"
BANFF CRAG AND CANYON, DECEMBER 15, 1900

Shanghai Shrimp

Henry Vultier, *Executive Chef*
BANFF PARK LODGE, BANFF

Serves 2

Shrimp, raw and headless 26 to 30 count	16
Vegetable oil	1 – 2 tbsp (15 – 30 ml)
Fresh ginger, peeled and thinly sliced	3 tbsp (45 ml)
Green onions, diced	3 tbsp (45 ml)
Dry sherry	2 tbsp (30 ml)
Soya sauce	2 tbsp (30 ml)
Sugar	2 tsp (10 ml)
Wine vinegar	½ tsp (2 ml)

Remove the shell of shrimp except for the tail and last section. Devein. Heat the pan and stir-fry the ginger and onions over low heat for 30 seconds, until there is an aroma. Add the shrimp and stir-fry over high heat for 1 minute. Add remaining ingredients and stir-fry until sauce is glazed, about 2 minutes.

Serving suggestion: Serve as an appetizer with fresh-baked sourdough bread to dip in sauce. Sprinkle with chopped fresh parsley just before serving.

Once again the Mounted Police are on the job in Banff and everybody is tickled... Banff citizens may now go to bed and snore as hard as they please.

BANFF CRAG AND CANYON, JULY 28, 1917

Vegetarian Burrito

Rudi Thoni, *Chef*
PAPA GEORGE'S RESTAURANT, JASPER

Makes 4

Tortilla shells	4 large
Refried beans, heated	14-oz (398-ml) can
Cheddar, grated	½ cup (125 ml)
Green onion, sliced	¼ cup (50 ml)
Sour cream	½ cup (125 ml)
Salsa	½ cup (125 ml)
Vegetarian Chili (page 101), heated	2 cups (500 ml)

Spread filling evenly over warm tortilla shells and fold.

While the Athabaska Depot was being built, Moberly worked his way down the valley and by Christmas was camped at Fiddle Creek. He has left an interesting description on his fare in Jasper on Christmas Day:

I paid a visit on Christmas Eve to the survey camp, to have a talk and smoke with the staff, some of whom were bewailing the loss of a dinner on the following day, so I invited them down to partake of the luxuries in my camp, about two miles away. My stores consisted at that time of some pemmican, flour and tea, without sugar. I had several courses prepared, the first being pemmican raw, the second pemmican boiled, and in due season the dessert, which was pemmican fried; and my guests looked somewhat disappointed when I informed them they saw all the luxuries before them, and the only thing we could do was to have a good smoke, as I had plenty of tobacco, and try to keep warm.

FROM *PACK SADDLES TO TÊTE JAUNE CACHE* BY JAMES MACGREGOR

Fresh Scallops *with* Beet *and* Red Cabbage Sauce

Gerhard Frey, *Executive Chef*
MOUNT ROYAL HOTEL, BANFF

Serves 6

Butter or margarine	4 tsp (20 ml)
Fresh scallops	18
Caviar	1 tsp (5 ml)
Salt and pepper	to taste

Melt the butter, add the scallops and sauté, but do not brown. Season lightly with salt and pepper.

THE SAUCE

Butter	4 tsp (20 ml)
Onions, chopped	2 tsp (10 ml)
Beets, chopped	2 tbsp (30 ml)
Red cabbage, chopped	2 tbsp (30 ml)
White wine	¼ cup (50 ml)
Fish velouté	1 cup (250 ml)
Beet brunoise (⅛-inch / 3-mm dice)	¼ cup (50 ml)
Whipping cream	2 tbsp (30 ml)
Baby beets, cooked	6

Melt the butter, add the onions and sauté lightly. Add the red cabbage and the chopped beets, sauté together for about 3 minutes and deglaze with the white wine. Reduce until almost all the wine is gone. Add the fish velouté, bring to a boil and simmer slowly for approximately 5 minutes. Purée in the blender then strain through a fine sieve. Bring back to a boil and add the beet brunoise and the cream, simmer for 3 minutes and add salt and pepper to taste.

To serve: Mirror the sauce on a plate, place 3 scallops in middle and top them with a few grains of caviar. Garnish each plate with a baby beet.

Veal Tortellini *with* Shrimp Cream Herb Sauce

Kevin Dundon, *Executive Chef*
LODGE AT KANANASKIS / HOTEL KANANASKIS, KANANASKIS

	Per serving
Veal tortellini, blanched	¼ lb (125 g)
Shrimp, cooked	½ cup (125 ml)
Cream herb sauce	½ cup (125 ml)
Parmesan and fresh herbs	for garnish

Heat pasta in a steamer and toss with butter, salt and pepper. Scoop pasta onto plate, add shrimp and ladle on sauce (below). Sprinkle with Parmesan and fresh herbs.

CREAM HERB SAUCE

Onion, diced	2 tbsp (30 ml)
Garlic clove, crushed	1
Butter or olive oil	for sautéing
Dry white wine	2 tbsp (30 ml)
Whipping cream	⅓ cup (75 ml)
Parmesan cheese	to taste
Chopped fresh herbs (basil, chives, parsley, oregano)	⅔ cup (150 ml)

For sauce, sauté onion and garlic in a little butter or olive oil until tender. Add white wine and cream and bring to a boil, reduce until thickened. Finish by adding grated Parmesan and fresh herbs, season with salt and pepper.

Tiger Prawns

Kevin Dundon, *Executive Chef*
LODGE AT KANANASKIS / HOTEL KANANASKIS, KANANASKIS

	Per serving
Large tiger prawns, peeled and deveined	6
Olive oil	1 tbsp (30 ml)
Garlic cloves, chopped	2
Paprika	pinch
Cumin seed	to taste
Coriander, ground	to taste
Sprig of rosemary	1
Cilantro, chopped	to taste
Lemon	½
Fresh ground pepper	to taste

Marinate the prawns in olive oil, garlic, paprika, cumin, coriander and rosemary for 12 hours. Place the prawns in a hot frying pan and sauté 1 minute. Finish with a squeeze of fresh lemon juice and chopped cilantro. Top with ground pepper and serve.

One kind of hypocrite is the man who, after thanking the Lord for his dinner, proceeds to find fault with the cook.

BOB EDWARDS' *SUMMER ANNUAL*, 1924

Mushroom Ragout *on* Four Colours

Gerhard Frey, *Executive Chef*
MOUNT ROYAL HOTEL, BANFF

Serves 6

Butter or margarine	2 tbsp (30 ml)
Onions, finely chopped	4 tsp (20 ml)
Various mushrooms, whole	2 cups (500 ml)
White wine	¼ cup (50 ml)
Salt and pepper	to taste

Melt the butter or margarine in a pan and add the chopped onions and mushrooms. Toss for two minutes. Deglaze with wine and season to taste.

SAUCES

Butter or margarine	2 tsp (10 ml)
Onions, chopped	2 tsp (10 ml)
Peppers, chopped (see note)	¾ cup (175 ml)
White wine	3 tbsp (45 ml)
Chicken stock	⅔ cup (150 ml)
Cornstarch	1 tsp (5 ml)
Whipping cream	3 tbsp (45 ml)
(mix cornstarch with cream)	
Salt and pepper	to taste

Sauté the onions and first colour of peppers on medium heat for 5 minutes. Deglaze with wine, add the chicken stock and reduce by ⅓. Put in a blender until all colour is gone from peppers. Bring back to a boil, add the cream and starch mixture and let simmer for 2 minutes. Strain through a fine sieve and season with salt and pepper. Repeat using the other 3 colours of peppers.

Note: You will make this sauce 4 times, using a different colour pepper each time: red, green, yellow and orange.

Lunch at Lake O'Hara, *1897*

Soups *and* Salads

Poppy Seed Lemon Yogurt Dressing

Jerry Cook
LAKE LOUISE STATION RESTAURANT, LAKE LOUISE

Makes about 2 cups

Kraft Miracle Whip dressing	1 cup (250 ml)
Plain yogurt	1 cup (250 ml)
Grated rind and juice of lemon	1
Poppy seeds	¼ cup (50 ml)
Parsley, chopped	2 tbsp (30 ml)
Cayenne pepper	pinch
Oregano leaves, whole leaf, rubbed	1 tsp (5 ml)
Liquid honey	1 tbsp (15 ml)
Fresh ground pepper	couple of twists

Mix all ingredients together. Stores well in the refrigerator for weeks. Can be thinned with a little water before use if dressing is too thick.

Miette Sulphur Springs ... One case worthy of mention was a man who was unable to walk when he commenced taking the treatment, but who in a couple of weeks was able to cover on foot the 12 miles of trail between the springs and Pocahontas. He stated that he had suffered from rheumatism for a number of years without being able to get any relief, but after a month's stay he was able to return home apparently entirely cured."

R.S. Stronach
ACTING SUPERINTENDENT OF JASPER PARK, IN HIS YEARLY REPORT FOR 1918–19

Raspberry *and* Balsamic Vinaigrette

Scott Schroeder, *Executive Chef*
LAKE O'HARA LODGE, YOHO NATIONAL PARK

Makes about 2 cups

Olive oil	1 cup (250 ml)
Balsamic vinegar	¼ cup (50 ml)
Raspberry vinegar	¼ cup (50 ml)
Red wine	¼ cup (50 ml)
Honey	3 tbsp (45 ml)
Dijon mustard	1 tbsp (15 ml)
Tabasco sauce	to taste
Worcestershire sauce	to taste
Salt and pepper	to taste
Lemon juice	to taste

Whisk all ingredients together and serve as a light dressing over fresh greens of choice.

Good old days on the trail ... When the coffee pot upset ... and the sugar and salt got wet and sometimes the beans went sour and the bacon musty and the wind blew smoke in your eyes ... how I wish I could live them all over again!"

Tom Wilson
PIONEER CANADIAN ROCKIES GUIDE, *BANFF CRAG AND CANYON*, MAY 1, 1925

Tarragon Salad Julienne

Michel Payant, *Sous Chef*
CHATEAU JASPER, JASPER

SALAD	Serves 4
Carrot	⅔ cup (150 ml)
Green pepper	⅔ cup (150 ml)
Green onions	⅔ cup (150 ml)
Hard-boiled egg	1
Butter leaf lettuce	1 head

Slice carrot and green pepper in symmetrical shapes. Finely chop green onions and egg. For each salad, layer the lettuce on the bottom, julienne of vegetables on top, then add dressing and garnish with green onions and egg.

DRESSING	
Mayonnaise	1 cup (250 ml)
Tarragon	⅓ cup (75 ml)
Honey	⅓ cup (75 ml)
Salt	to taste
White pepper	to taste
Water	3 tbsp (45 ml)

Mix mayonnaise, tarragon and honey in a bowl. Add salt and pepper to taste. Add water slowly and stir until well mixed.

Spiced Butternut Squash Soup

Scott Schroeder, *Executive Chef*
LAKE O'HARA LODGE, YOHO NATIONAL PARK

Serves 4

Butternut squash, seeded, peeled and chopped	3 lb (1.5 kg)
Olive oil	as needed
Brown sugar	to taste
Salt and pepper	to taste
Cayenne pepper	to taste
Onion, chopped	1
Carrots, peeled, chopped	2
Celery stalks, peeled, chopped	2
Garlic cloves, peeled, crushed	3
White wine	¾ cup (175 ml)
Vegetable stock	about 4 cups (1 l)
Salt and pepper	to taste
Whipping cream (optional)	½ cup (125 ml)

Preheat oven to 400°F (200°C). Spread pieces of butternut squash onto baking sheet and brush with olive oil. Sprinkle with brown sugar, salt and pepper and (sparingly) cayenne pepper. Roast until golden brown (about 20 minutes).

In a soup pot, sauté onion, carrots, celery and garlic in olive oil (brown slightly). Add white wine and cook for 1 minute. Add roasted squash and cover with vegetable stock. Bring to a boil, reduce heat and cook until all ingredients are tender. Purée in blender or food processor and strain. Return to heat, adjust consistency with more vegetable stock (if necessary). Season with salt and pepper to taste and more cayenne pepper (if desired). Add cream (if desired).

Chilled Fruit Soups

Scott Schroeder, *Executive Chef*
LAKE O'HARA LODGE, YOHO NATIONAL PARK

MELON SOUP — Serves approximately 4

Cantaloupe, totally puréed	2
Honeydew, totally puréed	½
White wine	1 cup (250 ml)
Triple sec	to taste
Nutmeg	to taste
Cinnamon	to taste

Combine all ingredients and chill.

BERRY SOUP — Serves approximately 4

Frozen berries (any combination of blueberries, raspberries, blackberries and cranberries. Cranberries give a good colour)	2–3 lb (1–1.5 kg)
Red wine	1 cup (250 ml)
Yogurt	¾ cup (175 ml)
Sambuca or Pernod	to taste
Honey	to taste
Chopped fresh mint	to taste
Water, if necessary	

Cook berries in red wine until soft. Purée and strain. Add yogurt, liqueur, honey and chopped mint. Chill well. Adjust consistency with water (if necessary). When serving, garnish with fresh mint sprig.

Variation: An interesting effect is created if both soups are poured simultaneously and slowly into flat serving bowls. If the consistency of the two soups is the same, it's easier to keep them from mixing together.

The establishment of the Alpine Club of Canada has already done a great deal to make the National Park attractive to lovers of mountain climbing. This club, which was organized at Winnipeg in March last year under excellent auspices, held its first summer camp at the summit of the Yoho Pass from July 9 to July 16. Over 100 members attended, and the proceedings were entirely successful. The situation was admirably chosen, only twelve miles from the village of Field, and at the same time in the heart of the mountains. The weather was perfect throughout, and Edouard and Gottfried Feuz, the Swiss guides in attendance, did their work most satisfactorily. Eight of the higher mountain peaks were successfully surmounted, Collie, the President, the Vice-President, Marpole, Michael's Peak, Wapta, Burgess and Field.

Howard Douglas
SUPERINTENDENT IN HIS "REPORT OF THE ROCKY
MOUNTAINS PARK OF CANADA" FOR THE YEAR 1906

Exotic Greens *and*
Prosciutto *with* Lemon Goat Cheese Dressing

Milos J. Moravcik, *Executive Chef*
INNS OF BANFF PARK, BANFF

SALAD	Serves 2
Roma tomatoes, vine ripened	2
Exotic greens	2 large servings

Use arugula, oak leaf, chicory, swiss chard, nicoise, dandelions—sold in some stores already mixed and bagged as California or field mix.

LEMON GOAT CHEESE DRESSING

Fresh goat cheese (St. Chevrier)	¼ cup (50 ml)
Lemon juice	2 tbsp (30 ml)
Lemon rind, very finely grated	1 tbsp (15 ml)
Mayonnaise	½ cup (125 ml)
Sour cream	⅓ cup (75 ml)
Fresh chives, chopped	2 tbsp (30 ml)
Garlic clove, minced	1
Light cream (10%)	2 tbsp (30 ml)
Fresh ground black pepper	½ tsp (2 ml)
Prosciutto, trimmed, lean, julienned	2 oz (55 g)

In a bowl, whisk the goat cheese and lemon juice until smooth consistency, whisk in lemon rind, mayonnaise, sour cream, chives and garlic. Continue to whisk while slowly adding the light cream until desired consistency. Season with salt and pepper to taste. Chill until needed. This dressing may thicken when refrigerated, just thin out with some additional cream.

Arrange the salad greens and Roma tomatoes on chilled plates, sprinkle with julienne of prosciutto and drizzle with lemon goat cheese dressing. Serve with slices of crusty French baguette.

Parsnip, Honey *and* Lime Soup

Tom Hayes, *Executive Chef*
BUFFALO MOUNTAIN LODGE, BANFF

Serves 8

Vegetable oil	2 tbsp (30 ml)
Small onions, diced	2
Parsnips	2 lb (1 kg)
Chicken stock	8 cups (2 l)
Honey	½ cup (125 ml)
Lime	½ cup (125 ml)
Curry powder	½ tsp (2 ml)
Salt and pepper	to taste

Sauté onions on medium heat until soft. Add peeled and chopped parsnips and stock. Simmer until parsnips are soft. Add remaining ingredients and purée in a blender or food processor. Adjust seasoning and serve hot.

Waterton: "inside lake," pukto-na-sikimi in Blackfoot, old name for Waterton Lakes which are inside the first range of the Rocky Mountains.

INDIAN NAMES FOR ALBERTA COMMUNITIES BY HUGH A. DEMPSEY, 1987

Green Chili Cilantro Vinaigrette

Greg and Neil Ronaasen
COYOTE'S DELI & GRILL, BANFF

Makes about 1 cup

Cilantro	¼ cup (50 ml)
Garlic clove	1
Green ortega chilies	2 tbsp (30 ml)
Cumin	½ tsp (2 ml)
Sugar	1 tsp (5 ml)
Salt	dash
Cayenne	dash
Red wine vinegar	2 tbsp (30 ml)
Orange juice	1 tbsp (15 ml)
Vegetable oil	¼ cup (50 ml)

In a food processor or blender, purée the cilantro, garlic, chilies, cumin, sugar, salt and cayenne. Mix in the vinegar and orange juice. Then with the processor on, very slowly pour in the vegetable oil until mixture is emulsified.

Banff: "holy springs," nato-oh-siskoom in Blackfoot, named for the hot springs; "waterfall place," minihapa in Stony [sic], and nipika-pakitik in Cree, named for the falls on Cascade Mountain; and: "in the mountains," tsa-nidzá in Sarcee.

INDIAN NAMES FOR ALBERTA COMMUNITIES BY HUGH A. DEMPSEY

Bumper's Beef Barley Soup

BUMPER'S BEEF HOUSE RESTAURANT, BANFF

Makes 15 cups

Water	8 cups (2 l)
Beef soup base	4 oz (125 g)
Barley	1 cup (250 ml)
Whole tomatoes, hand crushed	2 cups (500 ml)
Crushed tomatoes	1 cup (250 ml)
Tomato juice	½ cup (125 ml)
Onion, diced to ½ inch (1 cm)	1 cup (250 ml)
Celery, diced to ½ inch (1 cm)	1 cup (250 ml)
Carrots, diced to ½ inch (1 cm)	1 cup (250 ml)
Turnip, diced to ½ inch (1 cm)	1 cup (250 ml)
Beef, cut in 1-inch (2.5-cm) cubes and pre-cooked	½ lb (250 g)
Thyme	¼ tsp (1 ml)
Oregano	¼ tsp (1 ml)
Garlic powder	¼ tsp (1 ml)
Basil	¼ tsp (1 ml)
Worcestershire sauce	1 tsp (5 ml)
Bay leaf	1

Bring water to a boil in a 4-quart (4-l) pot and add the beef soup base. Warm barley with warm water to remove excess starch. Strain and add to pot. When barley is cooked about half through, add tomatoes, crushed tomatoes and tomato juice. Then add the diced vegetables, simmering on low heat until vegetables are about half cooked. Add beef cubes and spices and continue simmering until vegetables are well cooked. Remove bay leaf and serve immediately. This soup can also be cooled and reheated.

Scallop Salad *with* Balsamic Vinaigrette

Daniel Martineau, *Chef/Partner*
BAKER CREEK BISTRO, LAKE LOUISE

Serves 4

Romaine lettuce	1 head
Carrot	1
Red pepper	1
Lemon	1
Parsley sprigs	4

Trim and wash romaine, pat leaves dry with a cloth or use salad spinner. Rip leaves in strips 1 inch (2.5 cm) wide. Place romaine in 4 salad bowls.

Peel the carrot, wash and seed the red pepper, then julienne (cut into matchstick-size strips). Cut lemon into wedges. Keep aside the lemon, parsley, carrot and red pepper to garnish.

Olive oil	4 tbsp (60 ml)
Scallops	24
Salt	to taste
Freshly ground black pepper	to taste
Sweet basil	to taste
Balsamic vinegar	8 tbsp (120 ml)

Preheat a 10-inch (25-cm) pan on medium heat. Add the olive oil and scallops, then season them with salt, pepper and basil. Cook for 5–6 minutes or until done, when they are just firm to the touch. Overcooking the scallops will make them chewy. Then take the pan off the heat, pour in the balsamic vinegar and mix well. Spoon scallops and vinaigrette over the romaine, top with carrot and red pepper julienne and garnish with lemon and parsley sprigs. Serve immediately.

Mixed Salad *with* Tarragon Dressing

Claude Harvey, *Chef de Cuisine*
JOSHUA'S RESTAURANT, BANFF

MIXED SALAD

Mixed greens—Boston and butter leaf lettuce, endive, radicchio and spinach	
Tomato wedges, cucumber slices or orange wedges	for garnish

TARRAGON DRESSING — Makes about 1¼ cups

White wine vinegar	¼ cup (50 ml)
Olive oil	⅔ cup (150 ml)
Shallots	1½ tbsp (20 ml)
Garlic	2 tbsp (30 ml)
Lemon, fresh	to taste
Tarragon, fresh	1½ cups (375 ml)
Dijon mustard	2 tbsp (30 ml)
Salt and pepper	to taste

Place all ingredients in a bowl and stir well. Stir again just before serving.

Combine greens and toss with the Tarragon Dressing. Garnish the salad with tomato wedges, cucumber slices or orange wedges.

"I told my wife that if she bobbed her hair I would leave her." "But she bobbed it; and you're still living with her?" "You bet I am. I'll show her that she can't bluff me."

BANFF CRAG AND CANYON, MAY 1, 1925

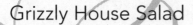

Grizzly House Salad

Phil Pappin, *Chef*
GRIZZLY HOUSE, BANFF

Butter lettuce
Radishes, sliced
Celery, diced
Carrots, shredded

Combine ingredients and toss with House Dressing.

HOUSE DRESSING	Makes about 2 cups
Mayonnaise	1 cup (250 ml)
Virgin olive oil	¼ cup (50 ml)
Honey	½ cup (125 ml)
Onion powder	1 tsp (5 ml)
Dill weed	2 tbsp (30 ml)
Paprika	2 tsp (10 ml)
Lea + Perrins	dash
White wine tarragon vinegar	¼ cup (50 ml)
Parsley flakes	1 tsp (5 ml)
Bay leaf, crushed	1
Dry mustard	1 tsp (5 ml)

Mix all ingredients well.

The good old Alberta dining room ... will on September 3, close its doors ... after that date there will be a number of hungry boarders, who frequently eat an awful lot and seldom very little, looking around for a new grub pile.

BANFF CRAG AND CANYON, AUGUST 18, 1917

Creme *de* Veau Chasseur

Markus Eisenring, *Chef/Owner*
PEPPERMILL RESTAURANT, CANMORE

Serves 10 at just under 1 cup

Veal, chopped and cooked	¼ lb (125 g)
Regular mushrooms, sliced	½ cup (125 ml)
Mushrooms, mixed variety (oyster, chanterelle, etc.), sliced	½ cup (125 ml)
Tomato, cubed	½ cup (125 ml)
Butter	1 tbsp (15 ml)
White wine	½ cup (125 ml)
Veal broth	9 cups (2 l)
Flour	6 tbsp (90 ml)
Whipping cream	⅘ cup (200 ml)
Salt and pepper	to taste
Lemon juice	½ tsp (2 ml)

In a saucepan sauté veal, mushrooms and tomato for about 2 minutes in butter. Add white wine and reduce a bit. Then add veal broth and bring it to a boil. Mix flour and cream together and pour into the soup. Let it simmer for about 15 to 20 minutes and spice with salt, pepper and lemon juice.

Queso Sopas (Cheese Soup)

MAGPIE & STUMP RESTAURANT AND CANTINA, BANFF

Serves 6 to 8

Chicken broth	3½ cups (850 ml)
Butter	½ cup (125 ml)
Green peppers, diced	¼ cup (50 ml)
Onions, diced	¼ cup (50 ml)
White pepper	1 tsp (5 ml)
Garlic powder	1 tsp (5 ml)
All-purpose flour	1 cup (250 ml)
Brick cheese, grated	½ lb (250 g)
Monterey Jack cheese, grated	½ lb (250 g)
Milk	to taste
Cheddar cheese, grated	

Heat broth. Combine butter, vegetables and spices in a saucepan over high heat and cook until butter is completely melted and vegetables are done. Add flour to butter–vegetable mixture and whisk rapidly until smooth and all butter is absorbed. Add heated broth and stir rapidly until butter–flour mixture dissolves. Let simmer on medium high heat until thickened. Add grated Brick and Monterey Jack cheese and stir in until smooth. Thin to desire consistency with milk. To serve, top with grated cheddar cheese and broil in oven until nicely browned.

Winter Squash Soup *with* Scallops

The Kitchen Brigade
RIMROCK RESORT HOTEL, BANFF

Serves 6 to 8

Butter	½ cup (125 ml)
Onions, chopped	2 cups (500 ml)
Squash, chopped (banana and corn)	2 lb (1 kg)
Chicken stock	9 cups (2 l)
Dry sherry	⅔ cup (150 ml)
Cream	2¼ cups (550 ml)
Salt and pepper	to taste
Scallops, sliced	6–8

In large pot, melt butter and sauté the onions. Add squash and sauté for 5 minutes.

Add the chicken stock and sherry then purée the mixture and pour back. Stir in the cream and season to taste.

Place the sliced scallops on a soup plate and pour the hot soup on top. Garnish with parsley and serve hot.

The village dogs seem to have vetoed the order-in-council forbidding them to run at large.

BANFF CRAG AND CANYON, AUGUST 22, 1903

Smoked Gruyère Cheese Salad

Kim Purdy, *Mt. Assiniboine Lodge Cookbook*
MT. ASSINIBOINE LODGE, MT. ASSINIBOINE PROVINCIAL PARK

SALAD	Serves 4 to 6
Romaine lettuce	1 head
Green onions, finely chopped	2
Celery, finely sliced	3 stalks
Apple, diced	½ cup (125 ml)
lemon juice	2 tbsp (30 ml)
Carrot	1
Cucumber	slices
Smoked Gruyère cheese, diced	½ cup (125 ml)
Sunflower seeds	¼ cup (50 ml)

Preheat the oven to 325°F (160°C). Toast the sunflower seeds in the oven for about 8 minutes, stirring occasionally. Remove from oven and cool. Set aside.

Wash lettuce and dry in spinner. Dice apple (leaving the skin on) and soak in lemon juice. Peel carrots, then make strips with the peeler. Prepare the other vegetables and toss everything together.

Add dressing to salad and garnish with sunflower seeds.

DRESSING

Olive oil	6 tbsp (90 ml)
Sherry or apple cider vinegar	3 tbsp (45 ml)
Dijon mustard	2 tsp (10 ml)
Maple syrup	1 tbsp (15 ml)
Garlic clove, crushed	1
Nutmeg	¼ tsp (1 ml)
Curry powder	½ tsp (2 ml)
Freshly ground black pepper and salt	to taste

Combine all ingredients well.

A cow is a female quadruped with an alto voice and a countenance in which there is no guile. She collaborates with the pump in the production of a liquid called milk, provides filler for hash, and at last, is skinned by those she has benefited, as mortals commonly are.

BANFF CRAG AND CANYON, JUNE 15, 1928

Belgian Endive *and* Oak Leaf Salad
with Pumpkin Dressing

Gerhard Frey, *Executive Chef*
MOUNT ROYAL HOTEL, BANFF

DRESSING

White wine vinegar	3 tbsp (45 ml)
Walnut oil	4 tsp (20 ml)
Sunflower oil	⅔ cup (150 ml)
Pumpkin, cooked and puréed	4 tbsp (60 ml)
Water	2 tsp (10 ml)
Sugar	1 tbsp (15 ml)
Salt and pepper	to taste

Put all the ingredients through a blender, then a sieve. Let the dressing rest overnight before adding the salt and pepper.

SALAD   Serves 6

Belgian endive	4 pieces
Baby oak leaf lettuce	6 heads
Mini pumpkins	6
Edible flowers	6

Use only the top of the Belgian endive (cut in half lengthwise) and mix with the washed baby oak leaf lettuce.

Cut off the top of the pumpkins and hollow out. Toss the salad in the dressing and arrange in pumpkins and place lids back on, covering ⅓ of the pumpkin. Garnish with the edible flowers.

Note: A very nice addition to the salad is thinly sliced smoked duck breast or poached shrimp.

Raspberry Vinaigrette

Jean-Luc Schwendener, *Chef*
MOUNT ENGADINE LODGE, KANANASKIS COUNTRY

Makes about 4 cups

Salad oil	3 cups (750 ml)
Raspberry vinegar	1 cup (250 ml)
Onion, finely chopped	1
Garlic clove, finely chopped	1
Mustard	1 tsp (5 ml)
Honey	2 tsp (10 ml)
Salt and pepper	to taste

Mix all ingredients well.

Man is a social animal, he loves to get in bunches of his own kind, and when ... people see that big crowds are coming to Banff, they say to themselves "the people are going to Banff," and away they go.

BANFF CRAG AND CANYON, SEPTEMBER, 1917

Grilled Belgian Endive Salad
with Scallops and Roasted Tomato *and* Garlic Dressing

Martin Luthi, *Executive Chef*
BANFF SPRINGS HOTEL, BANFF

DRESSING

Head of garlic	1
Roma tomatoes	2
Balsamic vinegar	¼ cup (50 ml)
Salt	pinch
Freshly ground pepper	to taste
Virgin olive oil	¼ cup (50 ml)
Chicken stock	¼ cup (50 ml)

Cut the top of the garlic head to expose the flesh. Wrap the garlic, without peeling, in tinfoil and bake in a 325°F (160°C) oven or on the BBQ until tender (about 1 hour). When done, squeeze the garlic out of the shells and reserve.

Cut the tomatoes in half lengthwise and roast with a little olive oil in the oven or on the BBQ. When done remove the skin and seeds and place together with the garlic in a blender. Add the balsamic vinegar, salt, pepper, chicken stock and slowly add the olive oil while the blender is running.

SCALLOPS — Serves 4

Large scallops	16–20
Skewers	4
Lemon, juiced	½
Virgin olive oil	4 tsp (20 ml)
Salt	pinch
Freshly ground pepper	to taste

Put the scallops on 4 skewers. Combine remaining ingredients and marinate with scallops for 30 minutes.

BELGIAN ENDIVE

Heads of Belgian endive, quartered lengthwise	4
Olive oil	2 tbsp (30 ml)
Salt	pinch
Freshly ground pepper	to taste
Butter lettuce hearts	
Oak leaf lettuce	
Chives	

Drizzle olive oil over the quartered Belgian endive and season with salt and pepper.

Preparation: On moderate heat, grill or BBQ the Belgian endive and the scallops for 3 to 4 minutes on 2 sides. Do not overcook. The endive should be crunchy.

On each of the 4 dinner plates lay out 3 to 4 butter lettuce hearts and oak leaf lettuce as a base. Place 4 of the warm Belgian endive on each of the plates and divide the scallops on top by pushing them off the skewers.

To finish the plates, drizzle the warm dressing over the salad and sprinkle with chopped chives.

The initial moonlight trip to Lake Minnewanka ... 60 ladies and gentlemen started out from the King Edward Hotel ... in Tally-hos, democrats, and buggies, a small orchestra also going out ... (to) the old chalet for supper ... after which dancing kept up till it was time for the return journey, home being safely reached shortly after two a.m.

BANFF CRAG AND CANYON, JUNE 25, 1912

Carrot Ginger Soup *with* Mussels *and* Scallops

Martin Luthi, *Executive Chef*
BANFF SPRINGS HOTEL, BANFF

Serves 6

Olive oil	2 tbsp (30 ml)
Young carrots, peeled and diced	2 cups (500 ml)
Red onion, medium, diced	½
Garlic clove, crushed	1
Ginger, fresh, peeled and sliced	1-inch (2.5-cm) piece
Scallops, large or medium	12
Mussels, in shell cleaned, washed	12
Dry white wine	½ cup (125 ml)
Chicken stock	5 cups (1.25 l)
Cream	½ cup (125 ml)
Salt and pepper	to taste
Plain yogurt	6 tbsp (90 ml)
Cilantro, chopped	2 tsp (10 ml)

In a saucepan heat up the olive oil on medium heat. Add the carrots, onion, garlic and sauté to a golden colour. Add the ginger, scallops, mussels and sauté for 1 more minute.

Add the white wine and reduce until almost dry. Then add the chicken stock and bring to a boil. When the mussels open, remove with the scallops and reserve. Simmer the rest until the vegetables are tender. Then place it into a blender, add the cream and blend until the soup is smooth. Pour the soup back into the pan, reheat and season with salt and pepper.

Divide the mussels and scallops equally into 6 soup plates and pour the hot soup over the seafood. Put a tablespoon of yogurt into the centre of each plate and sprinkle with cilantro.

Northern Mushroom Soup

David MacGillivray, *Executive Chef*
JASPER PARK LODGE, JASPER

Serves 4

Button mushrooms	2 lb (1 kg)
Butter	½ cup (125 ml) plus more for sautéing
Medium onion, finely diced	1
Garlic cloves, finely chopped	2
All-purpose flour	½ cup (125 ml)
Chicken stock	1 qt (1 l)
Dry white wine	1 cup (250 ml)
Honey	1 tsp (5 ml)
Whipping cream	1 cup (250 ml)
Rosemary, fresh sprigs	2
Salt and pepper	to taste

Wash and slice the button mushrooms, place on a towel and let dry before cooking.

In a heavy-bottomed saucepan melt the ½ cup of butter, add the diced onion and garlic and cook until lightly browned. Add the flour and incorporate completely and smoothly into the butter. Cook the roux for 2 to 3 minutes stirring constantly so it does not burn. Add your chicken stock and incorporate into the roux, being careful not to leave any lumps. The consistency should be smooth.

In a separate heavy-bottomed pot, melt some butter and sauté the mushrooms over medium to high heat. Once the mushrooms have cooked, add the wine to help remove all the goodness from the bottom of the pan. Once the wine has reduced by half add all the mushrooms, honey, whipping cream and rosemary to the soup. Season with salt and pepper. Simmer for 30 minutes on low heat.

Serve with Buttermilk Baking Powder Biscuits (next page).

Buttermilk Baking Powder Biscuits

David MacGillivray, *Executive Chef*
JASPER PARK LODGE, JASPER NATIONAL PARK

Makes 1 dozen

All-purpose flour	2 cups (500 ml)
Baking powder	2 tsp (10 ml)
Baking soda	¼ tsp (1 ml)
Salt	¼ tsp (1 ml)
Stick margarine, chilled, cut into small pieces	3½ tbsp (50 ml)
Low-fat buttermilk	¾ cup (175 ml)

Preheat oven to 450°F (230°C). Combine flour and next 3 ingredients in a bowl, then cut in chilled margarine with a pastry blender until the mixture resembles coarse meal. Add buttermilk, and stir just until dry ingredients are moistened.

Turn dough out onto a floured surface and knead 4 or 5 times. Roll dough to ½-inch (1-cm) thickness; cut with a 2½-inch (6-cm) biscuit cutter. Place on baking sheet and bake for 12 minutes or until golden brown.

If you like, you can add chopped fresh herbs such a basil, thyme or rosemary to the dough to give it a unique flavor.

It should be understood that the mattresses on the Bankhead rifle range were placed there for the use of the club members when shooting, and for no other purpose.

BANFF CRAG AND CANYON, AUGUST 11, 1906

Salad Eagle's Nest

Michael Clark, *Executive Chef*
SUNSHINE VILLAGE, BANFF NATIONAL PARK

DRESSING

Olive oil	3 parts
Balsamic vinegar	1 part
Dijon mustard	to taste
Peppercorns, cracked	to taste
Basil	to taste
Capers, chopped	to taste
Garlic	to taste
Salt	to taste

Mix oil and vinegar in mixing bowl and add enough Dijon mustard to emulsify the dressing. Add to taste the remaining ingredients.

SALAD

Radicchio lettuce
Butter lettuce
Pink grapefruit sections
Pine nuts
Diced red pepper

Toss radicchio and butter lettuce in dressing and arrange on plates. Fan out grapefruit sections decoratively along edge of plate, sprinkle pine nuts and red pepper on top of salad and serve.

Cold Corn Soup *with* Smoked Salmon

Mario Thom, *Chef*
LE BEAUJOLAIS, BANFF

Serves 10

Butter	½ cup (125 ml)
Onions, sliced	½ cup (125 ml)
Sweet corn kernels	28 oz (796 ml)
White wine	⅘ cup (200 ml)
Bourbon whisky	½ cup (125 ml)
Vegetable or chicken stock	4⅓ cups (1 l)
Whipping cream	1¾ cups (425 ml)
Sugar	⅓ cup (75 ml)
Salt and white pepper	to taste
Fresh dill	1 bunch
Puff pastry	½ lb (250 g)
Egg yolks	2
Smoked salmon	½ lb (250 g)
Russian caviar	1 jar

Melt butter in a skillet and sauté onions and corn. Stir in wine and whisky, then add stock, cream and sugar. Season with salt, pepper and fresh dill (re-serving some dill for garnish) and cook for 20 minutes. After cooling, blend and strain through fine sieve. Preheat the oven to 375°F (190°C).

While soup is cooling, roll out the puff pastry on some flour and cut out little figures (such as fish shapes), egg wash and bake for 3 to 4 minutes until lightly brown. After cooling, cut them in half and fill with a little caviar (like a mini sandwich). Before serving, garnish soup plate rim with smoked salmon and fresh dill, and place puff pastry figures in the middle of the soup.

Okonoki Salad

Robert Frost, *Executive Chef*
KILMOREY LODGE, WATERTON

Romaine lettuce	1 head
Tomatoes, diced	2
Avocado, diced	2

Clean and cut lettuce leaves into bite-size pieces. Toss in tomato, avocado and Saskatoon Vinaigrette Dressing.

SASKATOON VINAIGRETTE DRESSING — Makes about 1½ cups

Saskatoon berries	½ cup (125 ml)
Red wine	4 tbsp (60 ml)
Garlic	1 tbsp (15 ml)
Vinegar	4 tbsp (60 ml)
Olive oil	4 tbsp (60 ml)
Basil paste (see pesto, page 63)	1 tbsp (15 ml)
Sugar	2 tbsp (30 ml)
Parsley	1 tbsp (15 ml)
Salt and pepper	to taste

Combine all ingredients and purée in blender.

The only work done in the Waterton Park was the cutting of a good horse trail, six feet wide and six miles long, from Cameron Falls in the park to the International boundary line. Tourists can now ride through to the road in Glacier Park and the boundary line can be patrolled so as to prevent poaching from the American side.

Howard Douglas
COMMISSIONER OF DOMINION PARKS IN HIS "REPORT OF THE COMMISSIONER OF DOMINION PARKS" ANNUAL FOR THE YEAR ENDING MARCH 31, 1911.

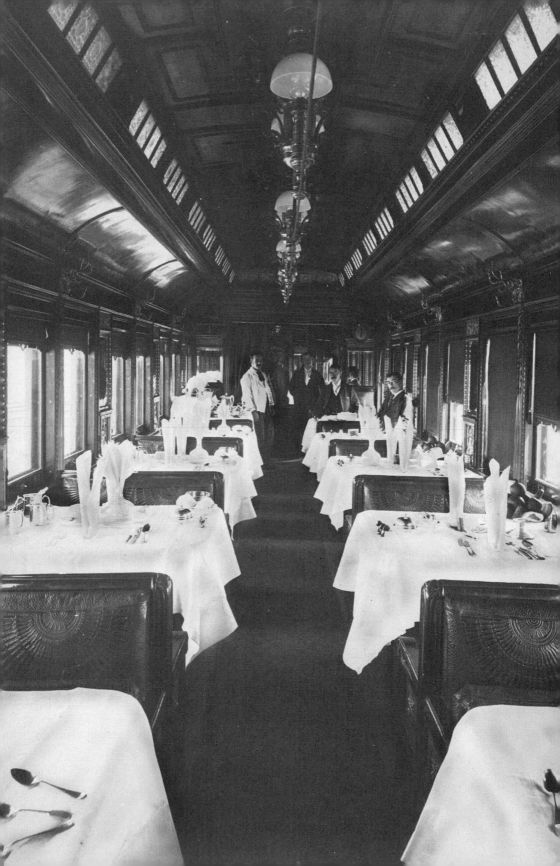

Entrées

CPR dining car Buckingham, *July 3, 1894*

Fresh Salmon Spiral *with* Sun-Dried Tomato Herb Butter

Scott Schroeder, *Executive Chef*
LAKE O'HARA LODGE, YOHO NATIONAL PARK

SUN-DRIED TOMATO HERB BUTTER

Sun-dried tomatoes	2 tbsp (30 ml)
Hot water	1 cup (250 ml)
Fresh thyme	1 tsp (5 ml)
Fresh basil leaves	5 – 6
Fresh rosemary	a few sprigs
Garlic clove	1
Salt and pepper	to taste
Butter	¼ lb (125 g)

Soak sun-dried tomatoes in hot water until soft, then drain. Process tomatoes, all herbs, garlic and butter in food processor to smooth consistency. Salt and pepper to taste then transfer to small piping bag with star tip.

SALMON   Serves 6

Fresh salmon, boned and skinned	1 side
Olive oil, as needed	
White wine, enough to cover	
bottom of baking dish	

Preheat oven to 400°F (200°C). Cut side of salmon lengthwise into ½- to ¾-inch (1- to 2-cm) strips and arrange in coils in a baking dish. Brush with olive oil. Season with salt and pepper. Cover bottom of baking dish with white wine then cover dish tightly with foil wrap. Bake 20 to 30 minutes. Transfer salmon to serving plates. Pipe butter onto hot salmon and serve immediately. Serve with rice and seasonal vegetables.

Option: Omit piping bag and refrigerate butter, cutting in pieces to serve.

Basil Sauce—Pesto

Mike Derondeau, *Owner*
GUIDO'S RISTORANTE, BANFF

Serves about 8

Grated Parmesan cheese	¾ cup (175 ml)
Grated pecorino Romano cheese	¼ cup (50 ml)
Fresh basil leaves, lightly packed	3 cups (750 ml)
Pine nuts or chopped walnuts	½ cup (125 ml)
Garlic cloves	3 – 4
Sea salt	½ tsp (2 ml)
Freshly ground black pepper	to taste
Extra virgin olive oil	1 cup (250 ml)

Grind the cheeses, basil, nuts, garlic, salt and pepper together in a food processor. Gradually add the olive oil until a thick sauce is obtained. Serve with your favourite pasta.

The sauce will keep if put in a sealed jar and refrigerated.

Variation: Add 2 tbsp (30 ml) of lemon juice or vinegar and 3 tbsp (45 ml) of oil and use as a salad dressing for cold pasta salad.

But, as fate would have it, someone had dropped a pat of butter on one of the two steps which lead into the room and, as happens once in every waiter's life ... (Oscar) and the fish went down together. To the not-so-dulcet sound of some not-so-polite snickers. Oscar pieced the fish together and proceeded to Reynold's table where he served the meal as best as he could with one arm—the other had been broken in the fall!"

AN EPISODE IN THE LIFE OF THE EXTRAORDINARILY DEDICATED 1920s WAITER OSCAR,
BY BART ROBINSON, IN HIS *BANFF SPRINGS: THE STORY OF A HOTEL*, 1973

Baked Chicken Breast
with Fresh Basil *and* Roasted Garlic

Scott Schroeder, *Executive Chef*
LAKE O'HARA LODGE, YOHO NATIONAL PARK

	Serves 6
Garlic cloves	6 – 7
Salt	
Olive oil, as needed	
Chicken breasts, boneless, skinless	6
White wine	¾ cup (175 ml)
Fresh basil, coarsely chopped	2 tbsp (30 ml) plus more for garnish
Butter	2 tbsp (30 ml)
Salt and pepper	to taste

Peel and crush garlic cloves (remove tough stems and sprouts). Place crushed cloves in a small ovenproof dish, sprinkle with salt, cover with olive oil and bake until garlic softens and begins to brown. Strain garlic out of olive oil, saving the oil. Crush garlic into a paste with a fork.

Preheat the oven to 400°F (200°C).

In a skillet brown the chicken breasts in reserved garlic oil, then transfer chicken to ovenproof baking dish. Deglaze the skillet with white wine and cook for 1 minute. Remove from heat and add roasted garlic and chopped basil. Stir in butter. Pour over chicken and season with salt and pepper. Cover baking dish with foil wrap and bake for 15 to 20 minutes.

Transfer to serving plates with a little of the baking juices and garnish with more fresh basil.

Can be served with Swiss Potatoes (recipe on next page).

Swiss Potatoes

Scott Schroeder, *Executive Chef*
LAKE O'HARA LODGE, YOHO NATIONAL PARK

Serves 6

Butter	to coat baking dish
Milk	1 cup (250 ml)
Whipping cream	¾ cup (175 ml)
Garlic cloves, peeled, crushed	2
Salt and pepper	to taste
Nutmeg	to taste
Cayenne pepper	to taste
Starchy potatoes (small, red-skinned potatoes)	about 8

Butter a 9 × 13 inch (22 × 33 cm) baking dish. Preheat the oven to 325°F (170°C).

Place milk, cream, garlic and spices in a medium saucepan. Peel and slice potatoes into milk mixture and heat on stovetop to boiling (milk and cream will begin to thicken with potato starch).

Pour into baking dish making sure all potatoes are submerged. Bake on the bottom rack of the oven for 1½ hours, until consistency is thick and creamy and top is lightly browned.

Scientists predict that in 100 years there will be nothing in the world to laugh at. But they're wrong because 100 years from now the people will laugh every time they think of us.

BANFF CRAG AND CANYON, MARCH 7, 1923

Vegetable Korma

Chris Montgomery
THE SHERWOOD HOUSE, CANMORE

Serves 6

Lentils (red or green)	⅔ cup (150 ml)
Vegetable oil	2 tbsp (30 ml)
Garlic cloves, finely diced	2
Onion, cubed	1 cup (250 ml)
Apple, peeled and finely diced	1 cup (250 ml)
Indian curry paste or powder	3 tbsp (45 ml)
Fresh ginger, finely chopped	1 tsp (5 ml)
Cardamom seeds	1 tsp (5 ml)
Unsweetened pineapple juice	2 cups (500 ml)
Coconut milk	14-oz (398-ml)
Tomato paste	1 tbsp (15 ml)
Mango chutney (any variety)	2 tbsp (30 ml)
Fresh lemon or lime juice	3 tbsp (45 ml)
Light soya sauce	½ cup (125 ml)
Fresh or dried chilies	to taste
Assorted fresh vegetables, cubed (see Note)	4 cups (1 l)
Salt	to taste
Corn or potato starch	1 tbsp (15 ml)
White wine or sherry	¼ cup (50 ml)

Note: For the vegetables, use your choice of what is currently available, such as cauliflower, carrots, celery, yams, turnips, potatoes, beans, asparagus, zucchini, mushrooms.

In a small pot of rapidly boiling salted water, cook the lentils until tender. Drain and set aside. In a large pot, heat the oil, and fry the garlic, onion and apple until translucent. Add the curry, ginger and cardamom and cook briefly, stirring to prevent the mixture from burning on the bottom of the pot.

Add the liquid ingredients and bring to a gentle boil. For hotter tastes, you may now add the chilies—the more you add, the hotter the Korma! Add the root vegetables from your selection and simmer until they are cooked "al dente." Then add the soft vegetables and greens from your selection, and the cooked lentils, and simmer for 10 more minutes. It is important not to add all the vegetables at the same time, to avoid overcooking and discolouration of the more delicate vegetables! Adjust the seasoning by adding salt or more soya sauce, and thicken, if desired with the starch mixed into the wine.

Serve accompanied with Patna or Basmati Rice, Raita (recipe follows) and Nan or Pita Bread.

RAITA	Makes 3 cups
Plain yogurt	2 cups (500 ml)
Cucumber, peeled and shredded	1 cup (250 ml)
Garlic clove, finely chopped	1
Onion, finely diced	1 tbsp (30 ml)
Fresh mint, chopped	1 tsp (5 ml)
Salt	to taste

Choose a good quality yogurt, preferably a "natural" variety. Remove and discard the whey (the watery liquid that has separated from the curd). Place the shredded cucumber in a fine sieve, and allow the juice to drain. You may add the juice to your Korma, if desired. Combine the drained cucumber, yogurt and other ingredients. Keep well chilled until time to serve.

Chicken Breast *with* Goat Cheese
and Sun-Dried Tomato Salsa

Milos J. Moravcik, *Executive Chef*
INNS OF BANFF PARK, BANFF

Serves 4

Chicken breasts, skinless, boneless (6 oz/175 g each)	4
Fresh goat cheese (St. Chevrier)	⅔ cup (150 ml)
Quark cheese	¼ cup (50 ml)
Garlic cloves, minced	3
Chives, finely chopped	2 tbsp (30 ml)
Freshly ground black pepper	½ tsp (2 ml)
Olive oil	3 tbsp (45 ml)
Salt	1 tsp (5 ml)

Place chicken breasts skin-side down on your work table, and with a tenderizer gently pound them out until they increase in size by ⅓. In a bowl mix together the goat cheese, quark, garlic and chives. Divide the cheese mixture among the 4 breasts and spread the cheese in the centre of each breast, leaving ½-inch (1-cm) border from the edge. Fold each breast over to seal in the cheese mixture and season with salt and pepper.

Heat the olive oil in a heavy skillet over medium heat, place the chicken in the heated oil and cook until golden brown, approximately 5 to 6 minutes on each side. Remove from pan and serve with a generous amount of sun-dried tomato salsa (recipe follows).

SUN-DRIED TOMATO SALSA

Makes approximately 3 cups

Sun-dried tomatoes, diced	½ cup (125 ml)
Red onion, diced	¼ cup (50 ml)
Jalapeño pepper, seeded and diced	1
Cilantro, chopped	¼ cup (50 ml)
Fresh lime juice	1 tsp (5 ml)
Rice wine vinegar	¼ cup (50 ml)
Tomatoes, diced	1½ cups (375 ml)
Garlic clove, minced	1
Sugar	½ tsp (2 ml)
Coarse salt	½ tsp (2 ml)
Freshly ground black pepper	⅛ tsp (.5 ml)

Mix all ingredients in a bowl. Allow salsa to set for 2 to 3 hours. Serve at room temperature.

The writer who wrote ... that the Canadian Rockies have the grandeur and beauty of the Alps, but lack the romance and poetry, has a long guess coming ... Regarding romance and poetry, it largely depends on the number of summer girls around."

BANFF CRAG AND CANYON, AUGUST 2, 1912

Salmon-Stuffed Chicken Breast

Jerry Cook
LAKE LOUISE STATION RESTAURANT, LAKE LOUISE

Serves 4

White unsliced bread	1 loaf
Sesame oil	1 tsp (5 ml)
Olive oil	2 tbsp (30 ml)
Garlic, finely chopped	1 tsp (5 ml)
Crushed chilies	½ tsp (2 ml)
Salmon fillet, boneless	1
Chicken breasts, boneless, skinless	4
Fresh parsley, chopped	2 tbsp (30 ml)
Freshly ground black pepper	1 tsp (5 ml)
Flour	1 cup (250 ml)
Thyme	pinch
Salt	½ tsp (2 ml)
Freshly ground black pepper	½ tsp (2 ml)
Eggs	2 to 3
Milk or cream	1 tbsp (15 ml)
Olive oil, for deep frying	6 cups (1.5 l)

The night before: Put the loaf of bread in the freezer to make it easier to handle. Mix the sesame oil, olive oil, garlic and chilies. Pour over the salmon. Marinate the salmon overnight in the refrigerator.

Make an incision about the width of two fingers into the thickest part of the chicken breast. (Put knife in and fan across and then pull out.)

Cut the marinated salmon fillet into four finger-size portions. Mix the parsley and pepper in a bowl. Roll the chunks of salmon in this to coat. Stuff salmon inside the incision in the chicken.

Mix the flour, thyme, salt and pepper together. In a separate bowl whip the eggs and milk or cream.

Take the bread out of the freezer and cut off the crust. Then cut the loaf into 3 pieces. Put through a hand grater, food processor or blender.

Coat the stuffed chicken with the seasoned flour and then the egg mixture and finally lightly pat in bread crumbs. Shake off excess. Heat olive oil in a wok or deep fryer to 400°F (200°C). There should be a light smoke coming off the oil. Put each piece of chicken in for 1 to 2 minutes until golden brown. Put on tray with paper towel to collect excess olive oil. Chicken can be refrigerated overnight or up to 2 to 3 days.

Bake in a preheated 350°F (180°C) oven for 10 to 15 minutes before serving.

Fettuccine with Tomato Basil Cream

Milos J. Moravcik, *Executive Chef*
INNS OF BANFF PARK, BANFF

Serves 2

Whipping cream	½ cup (125 ml)
Chicken broth	½ cup (125 ml)
Water	⅓ cup (75 ml)
Olive oil	¼ cup (50 ml)
Tomatoes, seeded and chopped	1½ cups (375 ml)
Fresh basil leaves, julienne strips	⅓ cup (75 ml)
Dried fettuccine	½ lb (250 g)
Freshly grated pecorino Romano cheese	2 tbsp (30 ml)
Freshly ground black pepper	1 tsp (5 ml)

In an large pan combine the cream, the broth, water and the oil, bring the liquid to a boil, and cook the mixture at a high simmer for 6 to 7 minutes. Add the tomatoes and basil and simmer the mixture for 1 to 2 minutes.

Cook fettuccine in a big pot of boiling salted water until "al dente" and drain well.

Place fettuccine in the pan with the sauce. Add the Romano cheese and coat the pasta well.

Apple-Marinated Cornish Game Hens

Tom Hayes, *Executive Chef*
BUFFALO MOUNTAIN LODGE, BANFF

Serves 4

Apple juice	4 cups (1 l)
Cider vinegar	1 cup (250 ml)
Calvados (an apple brandy from France)	¾ cup (175 ml)
Cornish game hens	4
Whipping cream	1 cup (250 ml)
Apples	2
Butter	2 tbsp (30 ml)
Salt and pepper	to taste

Mix apple juice, vinegar and Calvados. Split game hens down the back and remove back bone and wing tips. Spread open and flatten. Marinate hens in the apple juice mixture for 24 hours, turning occasionally.

Preheat oven to 375°F (190°C). Place hens skin-side up on a baking sheet and roast until done, about 30 to 35 minutes. Meanwhile, reduce 1 cup (250 ml) of the marinade with the cream to half of its volume. Slice the apples and sauté in butter. Serve hens on top of the sautéed apples and pour cream sauce over top. Serve with rice, barley or potato and vegetable.

The student of human nature will find many subjects of interest on the trails in and out of Banff.

BANFF CRAG AND CANYON, JULY 14, 1912

Hearty Moussaka

Tom and Maria Lambropoulos, *Owners*
BALKAN, THE GREEK RESTAURANT, BANFF

MEAT SAUCE	Serves 24 to 28
Ground meat	1½ lb (750 g)
Oil	3 tbsp (45 ml)
Onions, chopped	2–3
Garlic cloves, minced	3–4
Salt and pepper	to taste
Tomato juice	2 cups (500 ml)

Sauté ground meat in oil in frying pan. Add onions, garlic, salt and pepper, simmer for 10 to 15 minutes. Stir in tomato juice, simmer for at least 30 minutes.

CREAM SAUCE

Milk	4 cups (1 l)
Flour	¾ cup (175 ml)
Salt	1 tsp (5 ml)
Butter	¼ cup (50 ml)
Egg yolks	4

Pour milk in saucepan and stir in flour until dissolved. Place over medium heat and cook, stirring constantly until mixture comes to a boil and thickens. Stir in salt. Remove from heat. Add butter and stir well until melted. Add egg yolks, one at a time, stirring well after each addition.

FILLING

Potatoes	10
Eggplant	5
Zucchini	6
Oil	as needed
Salt and pepper	to taste
Meat sauce	
Cream sauce	

Peel and slice potatoes lengthwise. Slice eggplant lengthwise. Cut zucchini in long strips. Sauté vegetables separately in oil until lightly browned. Place on paper toweling in layers to drain well.

Preheat oven to 400°F (200°C). Cover bottom of 9 × 13 inch (23 × 33 cm) baking dish with layer of half the potatoes, season with salt and pepper, add layer of half the eggplant and layer of half the zucchini, seasoning each layer with salt and pepper. Pour meat sauce over top, spreading to completely cover zucchini. Repeat layers and seasoning, using all the vegetables. Pour cream sauce over top, spreading to completely cover zucchini.

Bake until vegetables are tender and sauce is golden brown.

Variations: Eggplant may be omitted if desired or moussaka can be made using only eggplant.

Canmore: "shooting at a young spruce tree," too-wup-chinchin-koodibee in Stony [sic]; when the Indians were camped on Canmore flats, young boys practiced by shooting at a young tree.

INDIAN NAMES FOR ALBERTA COMMUNITIES BY HUGH A. DEMPSEY, 1987

Caribou Loin *with* Peppercorn Crust
served with Red Currant-Calvados Glaze

Aaron Cundliffe, *Executive Chef*
EMERALD LAKE LODGE, YOHO NATIONAL PARK

Serves 2

Caribou loin	8 oz (250 g)
Salt and pepper	to taste
Dijon mustard	2 tbsp (30 ml)
Whole black peppercorns, crushed	1 oz (30 g)
Olive oil	2 tbsp (30 ml)
Red wine	2 tbsp (30 ml)
Calvados	2 tbsp (30 ml)
Game stock	¾ cup (175 ml)
Red currants	2 tbsp (30 ml)

Preheat oven to 350°F (180°C). Season caribou with salt and pepper, brush with Dijon mustard and sprinkle with the crushed whole peppercorns. In a medium saucepan heat olive oil until very hot. Sear the caribou in the hot oil. Remove from pan, setting pan aside, and place the caribou in an oven-proof baking dish and roast in the oven to your preference.

Pour excess oil from the pan you set aside and deglaze with red wine. Add Calvados and flambé. Add game stock and reduce until sauce is thickened. Add red currants, season to taste and pour over caribou loin.

Some hungry mortal made a raid on a cargo of beef … last night. Whoever was the culprit, he showed his epicurean propensities by leisurely cutting out the choicest bits.

BANFF CRAG AND CANYON, DECEMBER 29, 1901

Stuffed Salmon

SKOKI LODGE, BANFF NATIONAL PARK

STUFFING

Melted butter	¼ cup (50 ml)
Onion, finely chopped	1
Celery stalks, finely chopped	2
Garlic cloves, minced	2
Mushrooms, finely chopped	2 cups (500 ml)
Toasted almonds	½ cup (250 ml)
Cooked rice	2 cups (500 ml)
Parmesan cheese	½ cup (125 ml)
Sour cream	½ cup (125 ml)
Fresh dill and parsley, finely chopped	each 1 tbsp (15 ml)

Mix stuffing ingredients. Set aside.

HERB BUTTER

Soya sauce	2 tbsp (30 ml)
Garlic cloves, minced	2
Dill	1 tbsp (15 ml)
Melted butter	½ cup (125 ml)

Heat all ingredients of herb butter and set aside.

SALMON   Serves 6

Fillets of 12- to 14-inch (30- to 35-cm) salmon	6
Fresh lemon juice	

Preheat oven to 400°F (200°C). Place the stuffing on an oval ovenproof platter and brush with ⅓ of the herb butter. Drape the salmon fillets over the stuffing. Brush fillets with fresh lemon juice and cover with foil. Bake for 50 to 60 minutes, brush with remaining herb butter and garnish with lemon slices and parsley.

Canadian Mountain Stew

BUMPER'S BEEF HOUSE RESTAURANT, BANFF

Serves 6 to 8

Stewing beef, cubed	3 lb (1½ kg)
Flour	¾ cup (175 ml)
Beef gravy base	4 oz (125 g)
Water	8 cups (2 l)
Carrots, cubed	1½ cups (375 ml)
Celery, cubed	1½ cups (375 ml)
Onion, cubed	1½ cups (375 ml)
Turnip, cubed	1½ cups (375 ml)
Potato, cubed	1½ cups (375 ml)
Paprika	¼ tsp (1 ml)
Oregano	¼ tsp (1 ml)
Black pepper	¼ tsp (1 ml)
Basil	¼ tsp (1 ml)
Thyme	¼ tsp (1 ml)
Bay leaf	1
Red wine	½ cup (125 ml)
Whole mushrooms, canned or fresh	1 cup (250 ml)

In a large pot over high heat, brown meat until cooked completely through. Reduce heat to medium. Stir in flour and allow to cook into beef cubes.

In another pot, add beef base to water and bring to boil. Add to meat and stir until flour is well mixed in.

Skim off any fat or flour lumps from surface.

Add the vegetables, except for the potatoes, and cook on a medium heat until about half done. Add the potatoes and spices and simmer until vegetables are cooked through.

Then add the red wine and mushrooms. Simmer for about 5 minutes. If further thickening is desired, stir in a mixture of 2 tbsp (30 ml) flour and 2 tbsp (30 ml) red wine.

Remove bay leaf and serve immediately.

Crowds thronged the sidewalks and parking spaces for autos were difficult to find at times.

BANFF CRAG AND CANYON, MAY 25, 1928

Curry-Glazed Pork Chops

Lynne Grillmair, *Chef*
BUGABOO LODGE, CANADIAN MOUNTAIN HOLIDAYS

Serves 6 to 8

Pork chops, trimmed	8
Salt and pepper	to taste
Large onion, chopped	½
Cornstarch	1½ tbsp (20 ml)
Brown sugar	2 tbsp (30 ml)
Curry powder	1 tbsp (15 ml)
Cinnamon	1 tbsp (15 ml)
Salt	1 tsp (5 ml)
Water	1 cup (250 ml)
Beef bouillon cube	1
Ketchup	2 tbsp (30 ml)
Strained apricots (purée of drained canned apricots)	½ cup (125 ml)

Brown chops in a hot pan and season with salt and pepper to taste. Remove and lay in casserole dish.

Preheat oven to 350°F (180°C). Add a little oil to the pan and sauté the onion until translucent. Mix cornstarch, sugar, curry powder, cinnamon and salt together and then stir into pan mixture. Add water and cook until bubbling. Add bouillon cube and stir until dissolved. Stir in ketchup and apricots.

Pour over chops, cover and bake for about 45 to 50 minutes.

Serve with steamed cauliflower flowerettes with a light cheese sauce or garnished with buttered bread crumbs.

Broiled Chicken Breast
with a Strawberry Cantaloupe Salsa

Daniel Martineau, *Chef/Partner*
BAKER CREEK BISTRO, LAKE LOUISE

STRAWBERRY CANTALOUPE SALSA

Sliced strawberries	2 cups (500 ml)
Cantaloupe, ¼-inch (5-mm) dice	1 cup (250 ml)
Jalapeño, seeded and finely diced	1 or 2
Cilantro sprigs, chopped	5 or 6
Salt	to taste
Freshly ground black pepper	to taste
Tabasco	1–2 drops
Worcestershire	1–2 drops
Cayenne	small pinch
Limes, juiced	2

Mix ingredients in a bowl and let stand refrigerated for one hour.

BROILED CHICKEN BREAST · Serves 4

Olive oil	2 tbsp (30 ml)
Lemon juice	2 tbsp (30 ml)
Salt	to taste
Freshly ground black pepper	to taste
Oregano	small pinch
Basil	small pinch
Thyme	small pinch
Boneless chicken breast, trimmed	4

Mix the first 7 ingredients in a bowl then add the chicken and let sit for a few minutes. Preheat broiler and broil chicken breasts in oven for 6 to 8 minutes on each side. Top chicken with salsa and serve with Mexican fixings (rice, beans, tortillas, etc.).

Hunter Fondue

Phil Pappin, *Chef*
GRIZZLY HOUSE, BANFF.

Per serving

Vegetable oil	about 4 cups (1 l)
Buffalo	3 oz (75 g)
Rabbit	3 oz (75 g)
Venison	3 oz (75 g)

Heat vegetable oil in large, heavy fondue pot until hot but not boiling. Dice meat into 1-inch (2.5-cm) cubes and place on platter. With fondue fork, dip meat into the hot oil and cook to desire.

Serve with the following sauces.

ONION SAUCE

Mayonnaise	2 cups (500 ml)
White onion, puréed	½
Red onion, puréed	½
Bacon bits	¼ cup (50 ml)
Chives	½ bunch
White pepper	pinch
Onion powder	1 tbsp (15 ml)
Garlic powder	pinch
Lea + Perrins	1 tsp (5 ml)

MUSTARD HORSERADISH

Horseradish	½ cup (125 ml)
Dijon mustard, strong	½ cup (125 ml)
Mayonnaise	1 cup (250 ml)

BOURGUIGNONNE (HOT) SAUCE

Mayonnaise	¾ cup (175 ml)
Chili sauce	¾ cup (175 ml)
Cayenne	1 tsp (5 ml)
Tabasco·	1 tsp (5 ml)
Dillweed	1 tsp (5 ml)
Lea + Perrins	1 tsp (5 ml)
Brandy	1 tbsp (15 ml)

HONEY GARLIC

Mayonnaise	1½ cups (375 ml)
Garlic, crushed	½ cup (125 ml)
Honey	½ cup (125 ml)
Chives	½ bunch
White pepper	1 tsp (5 ml)
Dillweed	½ tsp (2 ml)

SWEET AND SOUR SAUCE

Fresh pineapple, blended	5 parts
White vinegar	1 part
Soya sauce	1 part
Ginger	to taste
Cornstarch	
Water	

Over a low heat, mix together 5 parts blended fresh pineapple, 1 part white vinegar and 1 part soya sauce in a small pot. Add ginger to taste, and water and cornstarch to thicken.

Chicken Breast Ticino

Markus Wespi, *Chef /Co-owner*
TICINO RESTAURANT, BANFF

Serves 4

Chicken breasts, double	4
Fresh goat cheese	½ lb (250 g)
Cream cheese	1 lb (500 g)
Green onions, chopped	½ cup (125 ml)
Egg yolks	2
Bread crumbs	1½ cups (375 ml)
Hazelnuts, ground	1½ cups (375 ml)
Eggs, lightly beaten	2
Salt and pepper	to taste

Preheat oven to 350°F (180°C). Clean the chicken breasts (take the skin off), open them to butterfly shape and pound well. Mix goat and cream cheese with chopped green onions and egg yolks. Season the chicken breasts on both sides and spread cheese mixture over one side. Fold the other side over. Mix the bread crumbs with ground hazelnuts, dip the chicken breasts in the eggs and bread them with the mixture. Brown the chicken breasts in a little butter on both sides and bake them for approximately 10 to 12 minutes.

Pork Tenderloin Dijonnaise

Markus Eisenring, *Chef/Owner*
PEPPERMILL RESTAURANT, CANMORE

Serves 4

Pork tenderloin	1½ lb (750 g)
Salt and pepper	to taste
Flour	for dusting pork
Oil	2 tsp (10 ml)
Butter	2 tsp (10 ml)
Shallots, chopped	1 tbsp (15 ml)
White wine	¼ cup (50 ml)
Whipping cream	1 cup (250 ml)
Sour pickles, small cubes	1
Dijon mustard, hot	2 tbsp (30 ml)

Slice pork tenderloin into 12 medallions, spice to taste and roll in flour. In a large frying pan sauté in oil and butter until done. Place medallions on plate and keep warm.

In the same pan sauté shallots then add wine, cream, pickles and mustard. Let simmer for about 2 minutes. Add salt and pepper and pour sauce over the medallions.

Serve with rice or noodles.

Banff is a playground set midst wondrous beauty, but Lake Louise is Beauty's Shrine ... the Mona Lisa of the Mountains."

BANFF CRAG AND CANYON, JUNE 15, 1928

Coconut Curry Chicken

Henry Vultier, *Executive Chef*
BANFF PARK LODGE, BANFF

Serves 2

Chicken breasts, skinned and boneless	2
Madras curry paste (available at well-stocked groceries)	2 tbsp (30 ml)
Olive oil	2 tbsp (30 ml)
Peppers, diced—use green, red and yellow	⅓ cup (75 ml)
Mushrooms, diced	2 tbsp (30 ml)
Onion, diced	3 tbsp (45 ml)
Port wine	2 tbsp (30 ml)
Chicken broth	⅓ cup (75 ml)
Tomato sauce, canned	¼ cup (50 ml)
Coconut milk	½ cup (125 ml)
Salt	to taste
Cilantro, chopped	1 tsp (5 ml)
Fresh lemon	½
Coconut, shredded and toasted	

Lightly salt chicken and baste with half of the curry paste. Quickly broil or pan fry to seal the chicken. (Chicken should still be pink when sealed). Slice chicken into strips about ½ inch (12 mm) wide, set aside and keep warm.

In oil, sauté peppers, mushrooms and onion until they are transparent but still crisp. Add port, broth, tomato sauce, remaining curry paste and coconut milk and bring to a boil. Reduce heat and simmer until slightly thick.

Stir in chicken and continue simmering until chicken is cooked, for about 2 minutes. If sauce becomes too thick, more broth may be added. Add salt to taste.

Just before serving, stir in cilantro and juice of ½ lemon.

Serving suggestion: Serve on a bed of white rice and sprinkle with toasted coconut. Garnishes served on the side may include chutney, pineapple pieces, raisins, chopped tomatoes or cucumber and banana slices.

Option: Curry paste can be substituted with quality curry powder—to taste.

You can't enjoy the most entrancing view or even be sociable with your fellow men if your stomach is full of say—burnt beans.

Harold Pripps
QUOTED BY ELON JESSUP IN *CAMP GRUB*, 1924

Eggplant Parmigiana

Barb Renner, *Mt. Assiniboine Cookbook, Mt. Assiniboine Lodge*
MT. ASSINIBOINE PROVINCIAL PARK

This is a meal in itself! Parmigiana takes time to prepare—like all good things in life! Count on at least 2 hours to prepare this dish. So pour yourself a glass of wine, turn on the music and pursue this culinary adventure! Some standard parmigiana recipes use ricotta cheese. This is a lighter version with low-fat cottage cheese and less salt. Double the portions to make an extra batch for the freezer.

Serves 4 to 6

2 small eggplants	1 lb (500 g) each
salt for draining eggplants	

TOMATO SAUCE	Makes about 3 cups
Coarsely chopped onions	1 cup (250 ml)
Olive oil	2 tbsp (30 ml)
Medium carrots, peeled and chopped	3
Canned whole tomatoes	14-oz (398-ml) can
Tomato sauce	14-oz (398-ml) can
Garlic cloves, chopped	2
Fresh basil OR	1 tbsp (15 ml)
Dried basil	1 tsp (5 ml)
Dried thyme	1 tsp (5 ml)
Cayenne pepper	¼ tsp (1 ml)
Bay leaf	1
Balsamic or apple cider vinegar	1 tbsp (15 ml)
Freshly ground black pepper	to taste

CHEESE LAYER

Low-fat cottage cheese	1 cup (250 ml)
Eggs	2
Chopped parsley	1 cup (250 ml)
Grated mozzarella cheese	4 cups (1 l)
Parmesan cheese	¼ cup (50 ml)

Eggplant preparation: Slice eggplants into ¼-inch (5-mm) rounds (don't peel it). Salt both sides of the rounds generously, laying the slices in a colander. (Eggplant is salted to remove excess moisture, which can be bitter. It also soaks up a great deal of oil when sautéed—salting can reduce oil absorption by two-thirds!) LEAVE SALTED EGGPLANTS TO SWEAT FOR 1 HOUR. You can make the tomato sauce and prepare the other ingredients while the eggplant sweats and drains.

Tomato sauce preparation: Brown the onions in the olive oil. Add the rest of the ingredients. Simmer for 30 minutes. Remove the bay leaf and purée the sauce in your food processor. Double this recipe if you want extra to freeze for spaghetti sauce, lasagne or gnocchi.

Cheese layer: Combine cottage cheese, eggs, Parmesan and parsley. In a separate bowl grate the mozzarella cheese.

Back to the eggplant! Drain and rinse the slices 2 to 3 times with cold water to remove all of the salt. Leave slices on paper towels to absorb moisture. Pat dry.

continued on page 90 …

Frying the eggplant: (Pour yourself another glass of wine at this point!) Heat 2 tbsp (30 ml) of olive oil in a skillet over medium-high heat for each batch of eggplant to be browned. (I use a measuring spoon to ensure that I don't use too much oil.) Lightly brown eggplant slices on each side. DO NOT ADD MORE OIL WHILE THE EGGPLANT IS COOKING. Remove cooked slices and place on paper towels to drain. Repeat until all eggplant pieces are done.

Assembling the final product: Preheat oven to 350°F (180°C). Spread 1 cup (250 ml) tomato sauce over the bottom of an oval 9 × 12 inch (23 × 30 cm) gratin dish. Arrange a layer of eggplant slices over the sauce. Top each slice with a spoon of cottage cheese mixture. Sprinkle 1 cup (250 ml) of mozzarella cheese over the layer. Arrange the next layer of eggplant so that it overlaps the first round. Add cottage cheese and mozzarella. After adding the final layer of eggplant and cottage cheese, spoon the remaining tomato sauce over the casserole. Sprinkle with the remaining mozzarella.

Bake for 25 to 30 minutes, until the mozzarella is browned and the mixture bubbles. If you have made extra parmigiana, freeze it uncooked. Before baking, unthaw it in your microwave.

 *Dress your duck and allow a slow cook to walk through a hot kitchen with it.*

Elon Jessup
COMMENT ON COOKING DUCK RARE 1924, IN *CAMP GRUB*

Fillet *of* Sea Bass *with* Fresh Mediterranean Herbs *and* Red Pepper Sauce

The Kitchen Brigade
RIMROCK RESORT HOTEL, BANFF

Serves 6

Red pepper, roasted and peeled	11 oz (300 g)
Salt and pepper	to taste
Shallots	2 tbsp (30 ml)
Butter	7 tbsp (105 ml)
White wine	1 cup (250 ml)
Fish stock	⅔ cup (150 ml)
Olive oil	⅔ cup (150 ml)
Fillet of sea bass	6-each, 6½ oz (180 g)
Fresh oregano, basil, thyme and marjoram	2 tsp (10 g) plus more for garnish

Purée red pepper in blender. Season to taste. Sauté the shallots in 1 tbsp (15 ml) of the butter, then add the white wine and the fish stock. Both liquids will reduce to half. Add the red pepper purée.

In a hot pan melt the remaining butter and add olive oil.

Season the fillet of sea bass with salt, pepper and herbs.

Saute the fillet on each side for 3 to 4 minutes. Remove from pan and keep warm in oven.

Pour some sauce on a warm plate and place the fish on the sauce. Sprinkle with herbs. Serve with vegetables and rice.

Lamb Loin *with* Pear William Sauce *and* Garlic

Gerhard Frey, *Executive Chef*
MOUNT ROYAL HOTEL, BANFF

GARLIC

Garlic cloves	4
Virgin olive oil	½ cup (125 ml)

Cut the garlic in fine slices (lengthwise). Heat the oil, add the garlic and fry until golden brown. Strain off the oil (use oil to fry the meat).

LAMB — Serves 6

Lamb loin, boneless	6-each, 5½ oz (160 g)
Salt and pepper	to taste
Olive oil from frying garlic	
Poached pears (for garnishing)	3

Season the meat with salt and pepper. In frying pan heat the oil and fry the lamb loins to your liking between medium-rare and medium-well.

THE SAUCE

Butter or margarine	3 tbsp (45 ml)
Pear, peeled and finely chopped	1
Sugar	½ tsp (2 ml)
Pear William liqueur	2 tsp (10 ml)
Demi-glaze	½ cup (125 ml)
Whipping cream	⅘ cup (200 ml)

Melt the butter over medium heat, sauté the pears and add the sugar. After the sugar is glazed, add the Pear William and flambé the pears. Add the demi-glaze and bring to a boil. Simmer for approximately 5 minutes. Lightly blend the sauce and strain.

Add the cream, bring back to a boil and simmer lightly for another 5 minutes.

To serve: Line each plate with the sauce and place the meat in the middle. Garnish each piece with ½ poached pear and sprinkle with the garlic. Serve with potatoes and vegetables.

—*Rev. Father Macdonald declares that Ike Mills' racing team is not composed of prohibition dogs as they show a fondness for light whines.*

BANFF CRAG AND CANYON, FEBRUARY 7, 1923

Beef *and* Veal Tenderloin *with* Madeira Sauce

Gerhard Frey, *Executive Chef*
MOUNT ROYAL HOTEL, BANFF

Serves 6

Beef tenderloin, one piece	1 lb (500 g)
Veal tenderloin, one piece	1 lb (500 g)
Salt and pepper	to taste
Oil (olive or vegetable)	½ cup (125 ml)

Preheat oven to 375°F (190°C). Season the meat with salt and pepper. On stovetop, heat the oil in roasting pan, and quickly brown the meat on all sides. Then roast in the oven to your liking. Ten minutes will give you medium beef and lightly pink veal. Take out of oven and let rest for 5 minutes before carving.

SAUCE

Red wine	½ cup (125 ml)
Veal stock (dark)	1¼ cups (300 ml)
Madeira	¼ cup (50 ml)
Cornstarch (mix with Madeira)	1 tsp (5 ml)
Salt and pepper	to taste

In a small pot, heat the red wine and reduce until almost gone. Add the veal stock and simmer for 5 minutes. Add the cornstarch mixture and simmer for another 5 minutes. Season with salt and pepper.

Chicken Breast *with* Tarragon-Yogurt Sauce

Jean-Luc Schwendener, *Chef*
MOUNT ENGADINE LODGE, KANANASKIS COUNTRY

	Serves 4
Chicken breasts	4
Butter or margarine	
White wine	¼ cup (50 ml)
Chicken stock	½ cup (125 ml)
Plain yogurt	4 tbsp (60 ml)
Tarragon, salt and pepper	to taste

In frying pan sauté the chicken breasts in butter or margarine until done. Remove and keep warm. Pour white wine in frying pan, then add chicken stock, together bring to a boil.

Lower heat and stir in yogurt, making sure it does not boil again, and season. Pour sauce over chicken breasts and serve on rice or noodles.

"I have a profound respect for bacon," remarked a thoughtful citizen ... "Did it ever occur to you that we are indebted primarily to bacon for the opening up and development and civilization of this great and glorious West? That without bacon, this grand country, with ... all its ... wonderful evidences of progress and prosperity ... would probably be a howling wilderness at the present moment?"

The thoughtful citizen paused for a breath.

"You astonish me," said his friend across the table.

FROM THE EDITORIAL "BACON AND CIVILIZATION," *BANFF CRAG AND CANYON*,
FEBRUARY 18, 1901

Char-Grilled Beef Tenderloin

Kevin Dundon, *Executive Chef*
LODGE AT KANANASKIS / HOTEL KANANASKIS, KANANASKIS

	Per serving
Beef tenderloin	5 oz (150 g)
Black peppercorns, crushed	
Balsamic vinegar	2 tsp (10 ml)
Extra virgin olive oil	¼ cup (50 ml)
Salt	to taste
Freshly ground black pepper	to taste
Asiago cheese	1½ oz (40 g)
Parsley, chopped	
Spring salad mix	2 cups (500 ml)

Coat piece of tenderloin heavily with crushed black peppercorns. Char-grill for 10 to 15 minutes, turning, once until rare. Make a vinaigrette by whisking together vinegar and olive oil. Season with salt and pepper.

Thinly slice the Asiago cheese and the rare beef tenderloin. In a large serving dish, layer lettuce, beef and Asiago. Drizzle vinaigrette over salad and garnish with chopped parsley and ground pepper.

Substitute for Asiago cheese: Parmesan cheese.

To have only a heavy club between one and a ton and a half of charging buffalo is no adequate protection.

BANFF CRAG AND CANYON, JULY 17, 1931

Veal Francesca

Michael Clark, *Executive Chef*
SUNSHINE VILLAGE, BANFF NATIONAL PARK

Serves 2

Veal escalopes (leg or loin)	8-each 1½ oz (40 g)
Seasoning salt	
Flour, seasoned to coat veal	
Butter	2 tbsp (30 ml)
Prawns, black tigers, peeled	8
Garlic cloves, minced	4
Sun-dried tomatoes, marinated Italian style	8–12
Parsley, chopped	2 tbsp (30 ml)
Green onions, chopped	3 tbsp (45 ml)
Lemon	1

Season the veal and coat with flour. Melt butter in a medium skillet until golden brown. Add veal. Sauté evenly on each side, then add prawns and garlic. Sauté until prawns start to turn pink and add sun-dried tomatoes, parsley and green onions. Sauté for 1 more minute and serve. Arrange veal on plates and top each piece with the sun-dried tomatoes. Arrange prawns on top of tomatoes and finish with a squeeze of lemon and the juice left in the pan.

Serve with your favourite garnishings.

... [the old mountain goat] was not cut down in the bloom of his youth; for though "K" pounded his steaks to jelly on the stones, and boiled and simmered his legs for hours, he failed to be "chewable" let alone digestible ... and no one of that party ever again sighed for goat.

Mary T.S. Schaffer
1911, IN *OLD INDIAN TRAILS OF THE CANADIAN ROCKIES*

Chicken Breast *with* Orange-Coriander Sauce

Martin Luthi, *Executive Chef*
BANFF SPRINGS HOTEL, BANFF

Serves 4

Fresh chicken breasts	4-each 6½ oz (180 g)
Salt and pepper	to taste
Ground coriander	to taste
Olive oil	2 tbsp (30 ml)
Garlic clove, crushed and chopped	1
Red onions	¼ cup (50 ml)
Carrots, ⅛-inch (3-mm) dice	¼ cup (50 ml)
Celery, ⅛-inch (3-mm) dice	¼ cup (50 ml)
Fresh orange juice	½ cup (125 ml)
White wine	½ cup (125 ml)
Strong chicken stock (instant or fresh)	2 cups (500 ml)
Saffron threads	4
Cold butter, flakes	2 tbsp (30 ml)
Cilantro, chopped	2 tsp (10 ml)

Season the chicken breasts with salt, pepper and coriander. Heat the olive oil in an ovenproof pan large enough to hold the 4 chicken breasts.

Preheat oven to 350°F (180°C). Sear the chicken breasts on all sides on medium heat until golden brown, then bake in the oven until done (approximately 20 minutes).

Remove the chicken from the pan and reserve in a warm oven. Add the garlic, onions, carrots and celery to the hot pan and sauté until tender.

Deglaze pan with orange juice and white wine and reduce to one third. Add the chicken stock and saffron threads and simmer until the sauce is reduced by half.

Whisk in the butter, adjust the seasoning and add the cilantro to sauce.

Cut each chicken breast into 4 slices and place on 4 plates. Spoon the sauce over the chicken and on the plate. Garnish with cilantro leaves.

There is not much to tell of my trip over Pipestone Pass. It was simply the case of a man starting on a seventy-mile snowshoe trip across the mountains to eat his Christmas dinner with his wife and family, and of getting there and eating the dinner, the pleasure being well worth the trip.

Tom Wilson
PIONEER BANFF GUIDE, 1909, CANADIAN ALPINE JOURNAL
(*AUTHOR'S NOTE:* FROSTBITE INJURIES FROM THIS TRIP LEAD TO
TOM WILSON LOSING PART OF SEVERAL TOES ON EACH FOOT.)

Fillet *of* Salmon Natasha

Michael Clark, *Executive Chef*
SUNSHINE VILLAGE, BANFF NATIONAL PARK

Serves 2

Butter	2 tbsp (30 ml)
Salmon fillets	2
Seasoning salt	to taste
Flour, seasoned with paprika to coat salmon pieces	
Red onion, finely diced	1 small
Green onion, chopped	4 tbsp (60 ml)
Parsley, chopped	1 tbsp (15 ml)
Basil, fresh	6 leaves
or paste	1 tbsp (15 ml)
Ripe tomato, diced	1
Lemon	1

Preheat oven to 400°F (200°C). Melt butter in a medium skillet until golden brown. Season salmon, coat with flour and sauté on each side. Place skillet in oven for approximately 10 minutes, or until salmon is just barely cooked. Remove salmon from skillet and onto plates.

In left-over juice, sauté onions, parsley, basil and tomato for 1 minute. Top salmon with mixture and finish with a squeeze of lemon.

Serve with rice and fresh vegetables of the season.

Vegetarian Chili

Rudi Thoni, *Chef*
PAPA GEORGE'S RESTAURANT, JASPER

Serves 8 to 10

Water	1 cup (250 ml)
Millet	¾ cup (175 ml)
Tomato sauce	14-oz (398-ml) can
Lima beans, cooked	14-oz (398-ml) can
Kidney beans, cooked	14-oz (398-ml) can
Corn, frozen	1 cup (250 ml)
Jalapeño pepper, minced	1 tbsp (15 ml)
Vegetable oil	2 tbsp (30 ml)
Onion, large, diced	1
Medium carrots, diced	2
Medium green pepper, diced	1
Garlic cloves, minced	2
Chili powder	2 tbsp (30 ml)
Tabasco sauce	dash
White pepper	pinch

Bring water to a boil, add millet and simmer until soft. In a large pot add tomato sauce, lima beans, kidney beans, corn, jalapeño pepper and millet. In a saucepan sauté onion, carrots, pepper and garlic until tender, then add to large pot.

Season to taste with chili powder, Tabasco sauce and white pepper. Let simmer for 10 minutes.

—Ⓓ *Jasper: "in the mountains," asinee-watsik in Cree, descriptive.*

INDIAN NAMES FOR ALBERTA COMMUNITIES, HUGH A. DEMPSEY, 1987

Elk Kilmorey *with* Saskatoon Sauce

Robert Frost, *Executive Chef*
KILMOREY LODGE, WATERTON

	Per serving
Elk steak	½ lb (250 g)
Clarified butter	2 tbsp (30 ml)
Saskatoon liqueur	4 tbsp (60 ml)
Shallots	2 tbsp (30 ml)
Saskatoon berries	¼ cup (50 ml)
Game Sauce	4 tbsp (60 ml)
Vanilla ice cream	¼ cup (50 ml)
Cream	4 tbsp (60 ml)

Sauté elk steak in clarified butter until medium rare. Remove steak and deglaze pan with Saskatoon liqueur. Add shallots and Saskatoon berries and cook until tender. Add Game Sauce. Add ice cream. Finish with cream.

GAME SAUCE	Makes 4 cups
Elk bones	1 lb (500 g)
Celery	½ stalk
Carrot	1
Onion	1
Water	9 cups (2.25 l)
Tomato paste	2 tbsp (30 ml)
Peppercorns	4
Juniper berries	4
Red wine	6 tbsp (90 ml)
Brandy	1 tsp (5 ml)
Cider vinegar	1 tsp (5 ml)
Salt	to taste

Brown bones in 450°F (230°C) oven for about 20 minutes. Add diced vegetables and brown 20 minutes more. Let cool for 5 minutes. Put bones and vegetables in stockpot and drain grease from roasting pan. Add 1 cup (250 ml) of the water and stir, scraping all bits and adding to stockpot. Add tomato paste and remaining 8 cups (2 l) of water or until bones are covered. Let simmer 4 hours then remove bones and vegetables. Add the rest of the ingredients and reduce by ½.

... she always moved with much grace, this charming waitress ... She waltzed in with a cup of tea, she waltzed out with an empty dish, and some of us got to keeping time with her motions ... we called her "The Waltzing Waitress."

Edward Roper
"ON DINING IN BANFF," 1911, IN *BY TRACK AND TRAIL: A JOURNEY THROUGH CANADA*

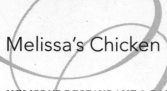

Melissa's Chicken

MELISSA'S RESTAURANT & BAR, BANFF

Serves 6 to 8

Eggs	2
Flour	
Boneless chicken breasts	1 per serving

Prepare egg wash by beating eggs in bowl. Lightly flour chicken and then dip completely in the egg wash.

In a hot frying pan, sauté the chicken in vegetable oil until golden brown on both sides.

SAUCE

Medium-size onion	½
Small tomato	1
Butter	4 tbsp (60 ml)
Flour	4 tbsp (60 ml)
Tarragon	to taste
Beef stock (or dissolve cubes of beef base in 5 cups of boiling water)	5 cups (1.25 l)
White wine	½ cup (125 ml)
Salt and pepper	to taste
Parsley	as garnish

Slice onion and finely chop tomato and sauté over a medium heat in butter for about 3 minutes. Add flour and stir until smooth. Add a pinch of tarragon and slowly stir in beef stock and white wine. Bring to a boil and simmer for about 5 minutes and add salt and pepper to taste.

To serve, place chicken on a bed of fluffy white rice and generously cover with sauce. Garnish with a sprig of fresh parsley.

Baked Salmon Fillet *with* Sesame Caper Butter

Barb Renner, *Mt. Assiniboine Cookbook*
MT. ASSINIBOINE LODGE, MT. ASSINIBOINE PROVINCIAL PARK

This is a very elegant, yet simple way to serve salmon.

SESAME CAPER BUTTER

Butter	4 tbsp (60 ml)
Green onions, finely chopped	2 tbsp (30 ml)
Sesame oil	1 tsp (5 ml)
Soy sauce	1 tsp (5 ml)
Capers	1 tsp (5 ml)
Sesame seeds	2 tbsp (30 ml)

Mix butter, green onions, sesame oil, and soy sauce together. Toast sesame seeds in the oven until lightly browned.

Add hot sesame seeds to butter mixture. Stir well. Pour the mixture on a piece of foil or waxed paper and roll into a cylinder. Place in freezer for half an hour.

SALMON   Serves 4

Salmon fillets	4

Place salmon fillets on a cookie sheet. Preheat the oven to 400°F (200°C). Bake for 15 to 20 minutes. The translucent flesh of the salmon will turn opaque once it is cooked (check by inserting a knife in the thickest part of the fillet). Do not overcook.

Remove sesame butter from the freezer. Slice rounds of frozen butter and place one on each fillet before serving.

Chicken Almondine *au* Curry

Michel Payant, *Sous Chef*
CHATEAU JASPER, JASPER

CHICKEN Serves 2

Chicken breasts	2
Salt	to taste
Pepper	to taste
Flour	⅓ cup (75 ml)
Large eggs	2
Milk	2 tbsp (30 ml)
Sliced almonds	½ cup (125 ml)
Butter	¼ cup (50 ml)

Preheat oven to 375°F (190°C). Season the two chicken breasts with salt and pepper. Cover both sides with flour and dip in egg/milk mixture and cover both sides with sliced almonds.

Warm up an ovenproof pan until it almost smokes. Melt the butter and fry both chicken breasts until golden brown on both sides. Finish by baking for approximately 10 minutes.

CURRY SAUCE

Small onion	1
Banana	1
Apple	½
Curry	2 tsp (10 ml)
Coconut, dried	⅓ cup (75 ml)
Water	1 cup (250 ml)
Chicken broth	1 cube
Butter	2 tbsp (30 ml)
Flour	¼ cup (50 ml)

Coarsely chop onion, banana and apple and pan-fry at moderate heat for 10 minutes. Add curry and coconut and simmer for a couple of minutes. Add water and when boiling add chicken cube, let reduce for 10 minutes.

Make a roux by melting butter, adding flour and stirring until well mixed. Strain the stock into another pot. When boiling again add roux to gradually thicken.

To serve, put sauce on each plate and place chicken on top.

—◯ I am told to consult carefully a food-value list ... for the good of my health ... Maybe if I did, I'd live to be a hundred ... Unfortunately, the camper is too busy to puzzle it out: one has to go fishing.

Elon Jessup
1924, IN *CAMP GRUB*

Herb Roasted Chicken

David MacGillivray, *Executive Chef*
JASPER PARK LODGE, JASPER

Serves 4

Chicken breast with thigh attached (boneless)	4
Fresh rosemary, chopped	2 tsp (10 ml)
Fresh thyme, chopped	2 tsp (10 ml)
Fresh basil, chopped	1 tsp (5 ml)
Vegetable oil, as needed	
Flour	
Fresh ground pepper	to taste
Salt	to taste

Pull back the skin of the chicken and rub the fresh herbs very generously into the flesh. Pull the skin back in place.

Preheat oven to 350°F (180°C). Heat a medium-size heavy skillet or electric frying pan. Add the vegetable oil and heat.

If you are using a coated (non-stick) pan, then you will have no problem with the skin sticking. If you are using a regular frying pan, then you can coat the breasts with flour just so it is lightly dusted. This will help in both browning the meat as well as keeping the juices locked in.

Brown the breasts in the oil and then season. You will finish them in the oven for about 10 to 15 minutes.

Serve with lemon wedges, new potatoes and asparagus.

Beef Stroganoff

Jaroslav Nydr, *Executive Chef*
CHATEAU LAKE LOUISE, LAKE LOUISE

Serves 6 to 8

Alberta beef, well aged	3 lb (1.5 kg)
Salt and pepper	to taste
Paprika	to taste
Oil and butter	for sautéing
Shallots, chopped	⅔ cup (150 ml)
Brandy	¼ cup (50 ml)
Mushrooms, quartered	¾ lb (300 g)
Tomatoes, chopped	2½ cups (625 ml)
Sour cream	1 cup (250 ml)
Lemon juice	1 tbsp (15 ml)
Whipping cream	1⅓ cups (325 ml)
Cornichons, julienned	16 oz (450 g)

Cut the trimmed beef into 1¼-inch (3-cm) cubes and season with salt, pepper and paprika.

In a deep frying pan, heat oil and butter and sauté meat, browning rapidly on all sides, keeping it medium rare. Remove from pan and keep warm.

In the same pan, sauté the shallots to a golden brown, stirring continuously with a wooden spoon. Deglaze with the brandy and add quartered mushrooms. Stir for a minute and add chopped tomatoes and half the sour cream and lemon juice.

Let the sauce reduce for a few minutes, season and finish with whipping cream.

When the sauce is ready, mix in the beef and ¾ of the cornichons. Do not let the sauce boil once the meat has been added (the meat will become tough).

Serve with rice pilaf and garnish with sour cream and the remaining cornichons on top.

Desserts
and Breakfasts

Fanny Fowles in costume, *c 1912*

Poppy Seed Cake

SKOKI LODGE, BANFF NATIONAL PARK

CAKE	Makes two 9-inch (23-cm) cakes
Poppyseeds	½ cup (125 ml)
Milk	¾ cup (175 ml)
Butter	¾ cup (175 ml)
Sugar	1¼ cups (300 ml)
Flour	2¼ cups (550 ml)
Baking powder	2½ tsp (12 ml)
Salt	½ tsp (2 ml)
Egg whites	4
Vanilla	1 tsp (5 ml)

FILLING	
Sugar	½ cup (125 ml)
Cornstarch	2 tbsp (30 ml)
Milk	1 cup (250 ml)
Egg yolks	4
Chopped walnuts	½ cup (125 ml)
Vanilla	½ tsp (2 ml)

ICING	
Stiff whipped cream	2 cups (500 ml)

Preheat oven to 350°F (180°C). Soak poppyseeds and milk together for 30 minutes. Cream together the butter and sugar. Sift together flour, baking powder and salt. Beat egg whites until stiff. Are all your bowls dirty yet?

Add the vanilla to the poppyseeds and milk, then alternately add with the flour mixture to the butter. Gently fold whipped egg whites into the whole mixture. Divide into 2 greased 9-inch (23-cm) pans. Bake for 25 to 30 minutes.

In a saucepan blend the first 4 filling ingredients together. Bring to a boil, stirring constantly, until smooth and thick then add the nuts and vanilla.

Spread filling between the 2 cakes and ice with the whipped cream.

Carl Rungius, the great animal painter of New York, was a guest this week at the King Edward. He then went north with Jimmy Simpson as guide. Jimmy will sure lead him into green pastures and beside still waters.

BANFF CRAG AND CANYON, AUGUST 4, 1917

Killer Pancakes

Greg and Neil Ronaasen
COYOTE'S DELI & GRILL, BANFF

Serves 4 Neanderthals
or 6 regular appetites

Large eggs at room temperature	3
Sour cream	1 cup (250 ml)
OR yogurt	¾ cup (175 ml)
OR buttermilk	1 cup (250 ml)
All-purpose flour	½ cup (125 ml)
Whole wheat flour	½ cup (125 ml)
Baking soda	1 tsp (5 ml)
Baking powder	1½ tsp (7 ml)
Sugar	1 tsp (5 ml)
Oil, if not using non-stick pan	1½ tbsp (22 ml)
Blueberries, fresh OR thawed	¾ cup (175 ml)
Butter	to taste
Maple syrup	to taste

Separate eggs and set whites aside. Beat yolks and add in the sour cream or yogurt or buttermilk.

Sift together the all-purpose flour, whole wheat flour, baking soda, baking powder and sugar. The whole wheat flour contains wheat germ and this will be left in the sifter. Save a few tablespoons of it to use on the top of the pancakes and add the rest to the dry ingredients.

Add dry ingredients slowly to the wet mix. Stir just enough to blend. Stir in oil if needed.

Using clean beaters, whip egg whites until firm. Fold whites into mixture and just combine.

Pour onto a hot pan (greased unless not-stick). Immediately place a few blueberries into each pancake. Brown on both sides. Serve, spread with butter and sprinkle wheat germ on top. Pour maple syrup over pancakes.

Variations: Substitute other fruits or a mixture of fruits. Can also be used as a waffle batter.

Clafouti

SKOKI LODGE, BANFF NATIONAL PARK

Serves 6 to 10

Butter, to coat pan	
Berries, of your choice	1½ cups (375 ml)
Milk	2 cups (500 ml)
Sugar	½ cup (125 ml)
Melted butter	2 tbsp (30 ml)
Vanilla	1 tbsp (15 ml)
Salt	pinch
Eggs	4
Flour	1 cup (250 ml)

Preheat oven to 400°F (200°C). Grease a Clafouti dish (oval and deep) and cover bottom with a layer of frozen or fresh berries.

In a large saucepan mix until warm the milk, sugar, butter, vanilla and salt. Remove from the heat. With a whisk, slowly add the flour and eggs, stirring constantly.

Pour mixture over the berries and bake for 30 to 35 minutes or until set. Serve warm or cold for breakfast or dessert.

Sweet Cheese Custard

Mike Derondeau, *Owner*
GUIDO'S RISTORANTE, BANFF

Serves 4

Quark cheese	1¼ cups (300 ml)
Sugar	⅓ cup (75 ml)
Whipping cream	½ cup (125 ml)
Small orange, grated peel	
Orange liqueur	1 tbsp (15 ml)
Fresh blueberries	2 cups (500 ml)
Fresh mint or chocolate shavings	as garnish

Blend cheese and sugar using beaters or a food processor. Add cream, orange peel and liqueur. Arrange fruit and custard in layers in a dessert glass. Garnish with fresh mint or chocolate shavings.

The custard will keep in the refrigerator for as long as the expiry date on the cheese and whipping cream.

Variations: Use any fresh berries—strawberries, raspberries, blackberries— or fresh apricots or melons. Can also use a different fruit for each layer.

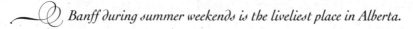 *Banff during summer weekends is the liveliest place in Alberta.*

THE MORNING ALBERTAN, JULY 15, "THAT'S LIFE FOR ME"

Pear William Fondue

Jaroslav Nydr, *Executive Chef*
CHATEAU LAKE LOUISE, LAKE LOUISE

Milk	1 cup (250 ml)
Sugar	4 tbsp (60 ml)
Vanilla bean	1
Grated lemon peel	to taste
Cinnamon	to taste
Cloves	to taste
Coriander, ground	to taste
Chocolate pudding	1 pouch
Whipping cream	⅔ cup (150 ml)
Pear William Schnapps	½ cup (125 ml)

Combine all ingredients in the bowl of your fondue set and heat on low until melted and smooth. Dip chunks of Comice pears and ladyfingers into the chocolate fondue.

... to give the trail-breakers a welcome, a bright idea popped into my head. "They shall have ... pudding." I made the pudding and we all tasted it and it was a good pudding, that is if it had been intended for a cannon-ball ... our campsite may fade, our trip forgotten, but that pudding ought to be there when the next explorers go through.

Mary T.S. Schaffer
1911, IN *OLD INDIAN TRAILS OF THE CANADIAN ROCKIES*

Strawberries Romanoff

Jaroslav Nydr, *Executive Chef*
CHATEAU LAKE LOUISE, LAKE LOUISE

Strawberries	1 lb (500 g)
Grand Marnier or substitute	5 tsp (25 ml)
Sugar	½ cup (125 ml)
Whipped cream	1⅓ cups (325 ml)

Crush the strawberries in the liqueur and sugar. Garnish with whipped cream and additional strawberries.

Royal Kir Granita

Milos J. Moravcik, *Executive Chef*
INNS OF BANFF PARK, BANFF

Serves 4

Fresh black currants	1 cup (250 ml)
Sorbet syrup (see below)	1½ cups (375 ml)
Champagne or sparkling white wine	½ bottle

Put black currants and the sorbet syrup in a saucepan and simmer for 5 minutes. Pass mixture through a fine sieve and let cool. Stir in the champagne and place mixture in the freezer until it forms an icy consistency. Remove from freezer, stir well and serve in tall parfait glasses. Great for hot summer days.

SORBET SYRUP

Caster sugar	1½ cups (375 ml)
Water	2 cups (500 ml)

Dissolve the sugar in the water over low heat, bring to a boil then cool.

Variations: Use raspberries, blackberries or blueberries.

Pear Tarte Tatin

Scott Schroeder, *Executive Chef*
LAKE O'HARA LODGE, YOHO NATIONAL PARK

Serves 8

Butter	4 tbsp (60 ml)
Sugar	¼ cup (50 ml)
Pears, peeled, cored and sliced	5 – 6
Cinnamon	to taste
Nutmeg	to taste
Pie pastry, rolled to 12 inches (31 cm), ⅛-inch (3-mm) thick	
Whipping cream, whipped	1 cup (250 ml)

Preheat oven to 400°F (200°C). On stovetop, in an ovenproof skillet, melt butter. Add sugar and caramelize (be careful as sugar burns very easily). Remove from heat. Add pears, sprinkle with cinnamon and nutmeg. Cover with pie pastry and with a paring knife stab through the pastry to vent. Bake 10 minutes then reduce heat to 375°F (190°C) and bake for 20 minutes.

Using oven mitts on both hands, remove from oven, invert large platter over skillet, turn skillet and platter over together so that tarte is now on platter, pastry-side down. (Watch for hot caramelized sugar that may leak over edges of platter.)

Cut and serve with whipped cream.

I am DEE-LIGHTED with your town.

Former US President Teddy Roosevelt,
VISITING BANFF IN 1915

Chocolate Pecan Tarte

Scott Schroeder, *Executive Chef*
LAKE O'HARA LODGE, YOHO NATIONAL PARK

CRUST	Serves 12 to 16
Butter and flour, to coat pan	
Pecans, coarse ground, roasted	1 cup (250 ml)
Chocolate wafer crumbs	1½ cups (375 ml)
Cinnamon	¼ tsp (1 ml)
Nutmeg	pinch
Butter, melted	⅔ cup (150 ml)

FILLING	
Semi-sweet chocolate	16 oz (500 g)
Whipping cream	2 cups (450 ml)*
Frangelico or Amaretto liqueur	¼ cup (50 ml)

TOPPING	
More roasted, crushed pecans	
Whipping cream, whipped, on plate when serving, to taste	1 cup (250 ml)

Preheat oven to 350°F (180°C). Butter and flour bottom of 9-inch (22-cm) springform pan.

In a mixing bowl, combine next five ingredients. Press into bottom of prepared pan. Bake for 8 minutes and cool completely.

Melt chocolate in double boiler. Remove from heat. Heat cream to just boiling. Whisk cream into chocolate until smooth. Stir in liqueur and cool slightly, stirring occasionally.

Pour chocolate mixture into cooled crust and tap gently on counter (removes air bubbles). Sprinkle more roasted, crushed pecans over tarte, and refrigerate overnight.

Serve small portions with whipped cream.

* *Note:* The usual equivalency for 2 cups is 500 ml. This recipe calls for the more exact conversion of 450 ml. This is to ensure that the filling will set properly. Too much whipped cream will make the filling too soft.

To preserve children: Take one large grassy field, one half dozen children, two or three small dogs, a pinch of brook and some pebbles. Mix the children and dogs well together and put them in the field, stirring constantly. Pour the brook over the pebbles and sprinkle the field with flowers. Spread over all a deep blue sky and bake in the hot sun. When brown remove and place in a bath to cool.

BANFF CRAG AND CANYON, JUNE 29, 1928

Caramel Hazelnut Pear Crumble

Marguerite Dumont, *Pastry Chef*
CHATEAU JASPER, JASPER

CARAMEL	Serves 8
Brown sugar	⅔ cup (150 ml)
Corn syrup, dark	1 cup (250 ml)
Butter	¼ cup (50 ml)
Whipping cream	1 cup (250 ml)

PEARS	
Ripe pears	4
Sugar	½ cup (125 ml)
Cornstarch	2 tbsp (30 ml)

CRUMBLE	
Hazelnuts	1 cup (250 ml)
Flour	2⅓ cups (575 ml)
Butter, softened	1 cup (250 ml)
Sugar	1 cup (250 ml)
Extra-large egg	1

In a medium saucepan mix brown sugar, corn syrup and butter. Cook until sugar is dissolved and butter melted. Add cream and cook until 235°F (112°C) on a candy thermometer. Cool until the mixture is still pourable. Alternatively, you can buy one packet of Kraft caramels and melt.

Peel and wedge pears. Mix sugar and cornstarch together. Toss pears into the mixture and let stand.

Roast hazelnuts on a cookie sheet until brown. Rub them with a clean cloth. The skin will come off easily. Put them in a plastic bag and crush them until they are coarsely chopped.

Preheat oven to 350°F (180°C). Put flour, butter, sugar, chopped hazelnuts and egg in a mixing bowl. Mix by hand or in a large mixer with a paddle until it looks like coarse crumbs. Butter a 10-inch (25-cm) springform pan and put a piece of wax or parchment paper on the bottom. Put half of the dough into the pan and drizzle ½ cup (125 ml) of caramel sauce over this bottom crust. Assemble pear segments onto caramel. Put second half of dough over pears.

Bake for ½ hour or until crumb crust is nicely golden. (*Special tip:* put cookie sheet on bottom shelf of oven to collect melted butter seeping out from sides of pan.)

Remove from oven, let cool 10 minutes and remove sides of pan while it is still hot.

Serve warm or cold with additional caramel sauce and ice cream.

A wise man once said: "Every one who has health and strength and is able to kick about the things that don't suit them ought to be satisfied."

BANFF CRAG AND CANYON, AUGUST 29, 1903

Chocolate Apricot Hazelnut Torte

Marguerite Dumont, *Pastry Chef*
CHATEAU JASPER, JASPER

APRICOT GLAZE	(can also use apricot jam)
Dried apricots	1 cup (250 ml)
Hot water	1 cup (250 ml)
Brandy	2 tbsp (30 ml)

CAKE	Serves 8
Semi-sweet chocolate squares	5 oz (150 g)
Butter	½ cup (125 ml)
Icing sugar	1 cup (250 ml)
Egg yolks	5
Vanilla	1 tsp (5 ml)
Egg whites	5
Flour	½ cup (125 ml)
Ground hazelnuts	¾ cup (175 ml)

FILLING	
Whipping cream	1 cup (250 ml)
Milk chocolate	9 oz (300 g)
Chopped hazelnuts	1 cup (250 ml)

COATING	
Apricot Glaze	
Whipping cream	1 cup (250 ml)
Dark chocolate	9 oz (300 g)
Apricot brandy	2 tbsp (30 ml)

Grease and flour an 8-inch (20-cm) pan and put wax paper on the bottom. Preheat oven to 350°F (180°C).

For Apricot Glaze: Cut dried apricots in half and let soak in hot water and brandy. Liquid will be used as a glaze. Set aside.

For cake: Melt chocolate in top of double boiler or use microwave method. Set aside. Beat butter with ½ cup (125 ml) sugar and egg yolks until light and fluffy. Add vanilla and melted chocolate. Beat egg whites with remaining ½ cup (125 ml) sugar until stiff peaks form. Fold beaten egg whites into butter mixture with flour and ground hazelnuts. Pour into prepared pan and bake for 40 to 50 minutes or until skewer is clean. Let cool on a rack.

For filling: Heat the cream in a small saucepan. Chop milk chocolate into small chunks and add to cream. Stir until all chocolate is melted. Remove from heat and add chopped hazelnuts. Set aside and cool. When filling is cooled and is thick put in mixer and beat until fluffy.

To assemble: Heat ¼ cup (50 ml) of the apricot liquid (glaze). Cut cake in half and place bottom half on a serving plate. Cover with apricot pieces and heated glaze. Pour chocolate hazelnut filling on top and then put second half of cake on top. Refrigerate until hard, about 2 hours.

For coating: Heat remaining apricot glaze with ¼ cup (50 ml) of water. Bring to a boil and stir until liquid. Glaze cake with apricot glaze.

Heat the cream. Add chopped dark chocolate, stir until all chocolate is melted. Add brandy and stir until mix is shiny. Remove from heat.

Spread coating evenly onto cake until it is a smooth finish. Garnish top of cake with remaining apricot and hazelnut.

Bumbleberry Pie

Tom Hayes, *Executive Chef*
BUFFALO MOUNTAIN LODGE, BANFF

CRUST	Makes 2 pies
All-purpose flour	5½ cups (1.375 l)
Salt	pinch
Lard or shortening	1 lb (500 g)
Egg	1
White vinegar	1 tbsp (15 ml)
Cold water	1 cup (250 ml)

FILLING	
Frozen raspberries	2 cups (500 ml)
Frozen blueberries	2 cups (500 ml)
Frozen strawberries	2 cups (500 ml)
Rhubarb, chopped	2 cups (500 ml)
Cooking apples, chopped	4 cups (1 l)
Sugar	2 cups (500 ml)
Flour	⅔ cup (150 ml)
Lemon juice	2 tbsp (30 ml)
Egg, beaten	1
Milk	1 tbsp (15 ml)

Mix flour and salt. Work in the lard until it resembles coarse meal. Whisk the egg, vinegar and water together. Add to the flour a little at a time until the pastry holds together. Wrap in plastic wrap and refrigerate for 1 hour. Roll the dough into two pie bottoms and two lids.

Preheat oven to 350°F (180°C). Toss all the filling ingredients together except for the egg and milk. Divide into the two pie shells. Top with pie lids, crimp together. Mix egg and milk together and brush on pie lids. Slit the tops with a paring knife to vent, and bake for 50 to 60 minutes, until golden brown.

Gelato *al* Caffe Ticino

Markus Wespi, *Chef/Co-owner*
TICINO RESTAURANT, BANFF

Serves 4

Egg yolks	3
Eggs, whole	1
White sugar	⅓ cup (75 ml)
White wine	¼ cup (50 ml)

Whip ingredients in hot water bain-marie or double boiler then whip over ice water until cold (sabayon consistency).

Liqueur (Triple Sec ½ part, Kaluha ¼ part, Brandy ¼ part)	½ cup (125 ml)
Instant coffee	1 tbsp (15 ml)
Hot water	2 tbsp (30 ml)
Whipping cream	1⅓ cups (300 ml)

Mix liqueurs with coffee diluted in water, combine with whipped cream and incorporate carefully into sabayon mixture. Fill into glasses or cups and freeze.

I put in all my conscience will allow then add a bit more.

Elon Jessup
ON MAKING CAMP COFFEE, 1924, IN *CAMP GRUB*

Apple Strudel "Mount Engadine"

Jean-Luc Schwendener, *Chef*
MOUNT ENGADINE LODGE, KANANASKIS COUNTRY

Serves 8 to 10

Apples (medium Red Delicious)	8
Sugar	2½ tbsp (40 ml)
Rum	¼ cup (50 ml)
Red wine	¼ cup (50 ml)
Lemon juice	2 tbsp (30 ml)
Hazelnuts, ground	⅓ cup (75 ml)
Cinnamon	1 tsp (5 ml)
Phyllo pastry	3 sheets

Preheat oven to 425°F (220°C). Peel and dice apples, mix with other ingredients and spread over phyllo pastry. Wrap to a roll, fold ends over and brush with water to keep moist. Wrap with second phyllo pastry layer and moisten again. Repeat with third layer and bake for 20 minutes.

The private distiller or moonshiner, call him what you will, was a wise and cautious man and had a habit of burying his surplus stock ... along the banks of Whiskey Creek. The liquid joy, no matter how it was distilled, should be almost priceless now ... whoever unearths (this) buried treasure should, in common humanity, donate a small portion (a gallon or two) to the editor of this journal — to be used for scientific purposes.

BANFF CRAG AND CANYON, 1916

Special Galatoboureko

Tom and Maria Lambropoulos, *Owner*
BALKAN, THE GREEK RESTAURANT, BANFF

Serves 10 to 12

Egg yolks	6
Sugar	1 cup (250 ml)
Fine Semolina	1 cup (250 ml)
Vanilla OR	
Rind of 1 lemon, grated	1 tsp (5 ml)
Milk	6 cups (1.5 l)
Phyllo	1 lb (500 g)
Unsalted butter, melted	½ lb (250 g)

SYRUP

Sugar	2 cups (500 ml)
Water	1 cup (250 ml)
Juice of 1 lemon	

Beat egg yolks and sugar together until well mixed. Add semolina and mix well. Stir in vanilla or lemon rind. Pour milk into large saucepan, heat until warm. Pour egg mixture into milk and heat, stirring constantly, until thickened. Set aside.

Preheat oven to 350°F (180°C). Place half the phyllo sheets in buttered medium-sized pan, brushing every second sheet well with melted butter. Pour in egg yolk mixture. Top with all but 2 of the remaining phyllo sheets. Turn all edges inward. Bake until golden brown. Remove from oven, let cool.

Combine syrup ingredients in saucepan, bring to a boil and boil for 5 to 7 minutes. Pour hot syrup over cold pastry. Cut into diamond-shaped pieces, serve immediately. Keep pastry at room temperature as it tends to harden if refrigerated.

Banana Rum Crêpes

Daniel Martineau, *Chef/Partner*
BAKER CREEK BISTRO, LAKE LOUISE

Make 6 to 8

Large eggs	2
White sugar	4 tbsp (60 ml)
Flour	½ cup (125 ml)
Milk	½ cup (125 ml)

In a bowl, whisk eggs and sugar until frothy. Add the flour and milk. Blend all ingredients to an even smooth consistency.

Cooking Crêpes: Preheat a 10-inch (25-cm) non-stick frying pan on a medium-high heat with one tiny drop of oil. When the pan is hot, lift with one hand while pouring in ¼ cup (50 ml) of crêpe batter. When the batter hits the pan, swirl it around so that it thinly and evenly covers the bottom of the pan. Your crêpes should cook quickly. When the crêpe is dry and coloured brown, flip it with a rubber spatula and cook it for 10 to 15 more seconds. Add a tiny drop of oil to the pan before starting each successive crêpe. Layer crêpes on a plate with wax paper between each one. Cover with Saran wrap and store in the refrigerator.

Note: If your batter doesn't spread easily when poured into the hot pan, it may be too thick. Whisk in a little milk and try again. Your finished crêpes should be thin.

CRÊPES FILLING·   Makes 4 servings

Butter	¼ cup (50 ml)
Bananas, sliced	4
Brown sugar	½ cup (125 ml)
Dark rum	½ cup (125 ml)
Water	½ cup (125 ml)

Melt butter in a 10-inch (25-cm) pan over medium heat, add the sliced bananas and cook for 2 minutes. Add the sugar, rum and water. Bring to a boil, mixing all the ingredients in the pan. Place the pre-made crêpes on plates. Have the crêpe slightly off centre, so that when you fold it in half, its edge is in line with the rim of the plate. Spoon the bananas onto one half of the crêpe and fold the outside edge over the filling. Pour the remaining sauce over the crêpes and serve with ice cream or whipped cream. For colour, garnish with fresh fruit and a mint sprig.

High up on rocky or snowy slopes one may hear, too, a sharp little nasal bleat and, turning, discover a small greyish animal, about the size of a Guinea pig, with rounded ears, short legs and no visible tail, running rabbit-like across the boulders. This is the pika, cony, or little chief hare of the mountains, also called "the haymaker" from his curious habit of storing away dried grasses and plants for his winter food. Sometimes under an overhanging rock there will be found his miniature haystack, a bundle containing perhaps a bushel of well cured vegetation which includes apparently every plant in the neighbourhood.

"ON ROCKY MOUNTAIN PIKA" FROM *JASPER NATIONAL PARK* BY M.B. WILLIAMS

Chocolate Mousse Cake

Jan Hrabec
JOSHUA'S RESTAURANT, BANFF

Makes 1 cake

Gelatine sheets	6
Chocolate (semi-sweet)	14 oz (400 g)
Whipping cream	3 cups (750 ml)
Egg whites	4
Sponge cakes	enough to line a spring form pan

Melt gelatine and fold into the melted chocolate. In separate bowls whip the cream until stiff and also beat egg whites until stiff peaks form.

Fold whipping cream into chocolate then fold egg whites into chocolate/cream mixture.

Place a layer of sponge cakes in a 10-inch (25-cm) springform pan and pour mousse mixture on top. Allow to set. Glaze with following ganache.

GANACHE

Chocolate	14 oz (400 g)
Whipping cream	1½ cups (375 ml)

Melt in hot water bain-marie or double boiler and glaze chocolate mousse cake.

"I wish to complain," said the bride haughtily, "about that flour you sold me, It was tough." "Tough, ma'am?" asked the grocer. "Yes tough. I made a pie with it and my husband could hardly cut it."

BANFF CRAG AND CANYON, AUGUST 24, 1912

Berries Gratin

Markus Eisenring, *Chef/Owner*
PEPPERMILL RESTAURANT, CANMORE

	Serves 4
Mixed berries	½ lb (250 g)
Sugar	1 tsp (5 ml)
Kirsch	¼ cup (50 ml)
Egg yolks	4
Sugar	2 tbsp (30 ml)
Kirsch	¼ cup (50 ml)
Vanilla extract	1 tsp (5 ml)
Whipping cream	⅔ cup (150 ml)
Icing sugar	to finish

In a bowl, marinate berries with 1 tsp. (5 ml) sugar and the Kirsch. Place berries in a gratin form.

Preheat oven to 400°F (200°C). Mix egg yolks, sugar, Kirsch and vanilla extract and beat until creamy.

Whip cream and fold in the creamy egg and sugar mixture.

Pour over the berries and bake for 30 to 40 minutes or until browned. Sprinkle with icing sugar and serve with pistachio ice cream.

Balloon jumping is the newest sport in England. You attach a small balloon to yourself and it makes you so buoyant that you can jump over barns, haystacks, and trees with ease.

BANFF CRAG AND CANYON, MAY 8, 1925

Carrot Cake

Chris McKercher, *Pastry Chef*
BANFF PARK LODGE, BANFF

Makes 1 cake

Crushed, canned pineapple, drained (reserve juice)	1 cup (250 ml)
Raisins	½ cup (125 ml)
Carrots, grated and lightly packed	¾ cup (175 ml)
Granulated sugar	2 cups (500 ml)
All-purpose flour	2⅓ cups (575 ml)
Baking soda	2 tsp (10 ml)
Cinnamon	5 tsp (25 ml)
Allspice	1 tbsp (15 ml)
Nutmeg	2 tsp (10 ml)
Eggs, large	3
Oil	1 cup (250 ml)
Vanilla	1½ tsp (7 ml)

Grease and flour a 9 × 13 inch (23 × 33 cm) cake pan. Drain pineapple well, saving the juice. Boil raisins in pineapple juice, drain and set aside. Place pineapple, raisins and carrots in a bowl.

Preheat oven to 350°F (180°C). Combine all dry ingredients in mixing bowl, blend in eggs, oil and vanilla. Mixture will be thick.

Add pineapple, carrots and raisins and mix well. Pour mixture into prepared pan and bake for 30 to 45 minutes.

When cool, cover with cream cheese icing.

Cream cheese (do not use soft, spreadable cream cheese)	12 oz (375 g)
Icing sugar	1 cup (250 ml)
Butter, melted but not hot	½ cup (125 ml)

Blend cream cheese with icing sugar. Add the melted butter and mix very well.

Sunburst Plum Cake

Sandra Howard, *Mt. Assiniboine Lodge Cookbook*
MT. ASSINIBOINE LODGE, MT. ASSINIBOINE PROVINCIAL PARK

Makes 1 cake

Butter or margarine	¾ cup (175 ml)
White sugar	¾ cup (175 ml)
Eggs	4
Vanilla	1½ tsp (7 ml)
White flour	1½ cups (375 ml)
Baking powder	1 tsp (5 ml)
Fruit (see Note)	

Note: For fruit use fresh plums or peaches, sliced in wedges, or one 28-oz (796-ml) can of peaches, drained and blotted dry, cut in wedges.

Preheat Cream butter and sugar until light. Beat in eggs, one at a time, then add vanilla. Mix flour with baking powder and add to egg mixture. The batter will be quite thick. Spread batter in an 11-inch (28-cm) fluted flan pan. Arrange sliced fruit on top of batter—press in lightly.

Bake for 25 to 30 minutes. Serve with light cream.

Crème Brûlée

Sandra Eichenberger
LE BEAUJOLAIS, BANFF

Serves 10

Sugar	1 cup (250 ml)
Milk	4⅓ cups (1 l) *
Eggs	2
Custard powder	2 tbsp (30 g)
Whipping cream	⅘ cup (200 ml)

Caramelize sugar in a pan and carefully add 4 cups (900 ml) of milk. Cook for a moment.

In a separate bowl mix eggs, custard powder and remaining ⅓ cup (100 ml) milk together and add to the sugar–milk mixture. Again, cook for a moment and set aside.

After cooling, add whipped cream and serve with cookies.

* A slightly different equivalency is used here than standard, for accuracy.

The ignorant imbecile who contributed the Banff items to the (Calgary) Albertan of Saturday's issue may be surprised that his identity is well known, and his cowardly remarks regarding the lady members of the Banff Quadrille Club will but intensify the supreme contempt in which he is already held. The editor of this paper will take pleasure in assisting the ladies to administer to this sneaking reptile the only punishment his miserable apology for a soul is capable of appreciating—a good horse-whipping.

BANFF CRAG AND CANYON, FEBRUARY 2, 1901

Fruit *and* Buttermilk Pancakes

Trudi Wagler-Bowman, *Mt. Assiniboine Lodge Cookbook*
MT. ASSINIBOINE LODGE, MT. ASSINIBOINE PROVINCIAL PARK

Makes about
2 dozen pancakes

Buttermilk or yogurt	1 cup (250 ml)
Sunflower oil	2 tbsp (30 ml)
White sugar	1 tbsp (15 ml)
Eggs	2
White flour	½ cup (125 ml)
Whole wheat flour	½ cup (125 ml)
Wheat germ	¼ cup (50 ml)
Baking powder	1 tsp (5 ml)
Baking soda	½ tsp (2 ml)
Salt	pinch
Fresh fruit (grated apple, sliced peaches, bananas or fresh strawberries and sliced banana)	½–1 cup (125–250 ml)

Beat first 3 ingredients together. Add second group of ingredients mixing only until thoroughly moistened. If the batter is too thick, add 2 to 3 tbsp. (30 to 45 ml) milk. Gently stir in the fresh fruit.

Fry on a hot greased skillet. Serve with yogurt, honey or maple syrup.

... the Banff Literary-Dramatic Club ... was quite annoyed at certain individuals who persisted in laughing and snickering during the presentation of "The Riders of the Sea"—a most dramatic play, depicting the morbid customs of the Irish fisher folk ...

BANFF CRAG AND CANYON, APRIL 24, 1923

Fresh Fruit *and* Berry Timbale
with Grand Marnier Ice Cream

Gerhard Frey, *Executive Chef*
MOUNT ROYAL HOTEL, BANFF

Serves 6

Bite-size sponge cakes	18
Mixed fruit and berries of your choice, cut into small pieces	
Sugar syrup	6 tbsp (90 ml)
Puff pastry circles ⅛-inch (3-mm) thick and 1-inch (2.5-cm) larger then opening of cup	6
Egg, lightly beaten	1
Sugar	2 tsp (10 ml)

Preheat oven to 340°F (175°C). Place 3 sponge cakes in each of 6 ovenproof cups. In a bowl mix the fruit and berries with the sugar syrup and fill the cups with the mixture. Brush one side of the pastry circles with the egg. Place brushed side down on cups and fold the pastry over the edge, sealing cups. Brush the top with remaining egg and sprinkle with the sugar. Bake for approximately 15 minutes, until golden brown.

GRAND MARNIER ICE CREAM

Milk	1¾ cups (425 ml)
Sugar	½ cup (125 ml)
Egg yolks	4
Whipping cream	½ cup (125 ml)
Grand Marnier	¼ cup (50 ml)
Orange zest, finely chopped, from 2 oranges	

Bring milk to a boil. Combine sugar and eggs in a bowl. Slowly add the boiled milk to the egg and sugar mixture, whisking constantly. Return to pot and heat until slightly thickened without boiling. Remove from heat, add the cream, Grand Marnier and the zest. Let cool in refrigerator for 2 hours then freeze in ice cream maker.

To serve: With the timbale fresh out of the oven, serve one scoop of ice cream on the side. At the table, cut off the pastry lid and place the ice cream on top of the fruit.

In the true chef's tradition he threw pots and pans around the kitchen, hurled carving knives at helpers ... (in a rage and) Brandishing a large spoon he ... vaulted over ... the counter—to land ... right in the middle of 360 dessert dishes of jello, each topped with whipped cream and one-quarter of a maraschino cherry.

DESCRIPTION OF 1920s CHEF ROBERT, BY BART ROBINSON, IN HIS *BANFF SPRINGS: THE STORY OF A HOTEL*, 1973

Chocolate Decadent Cake

Kevin Dundon, *Executive Chef*
LODGE AT KANANASKIS / HOTEL KANANASKIS, KANANASKIS

This dense, flourless cake is really a cross between chocolate mousse and pâté. Delicious and definitely decadent!

BROWNIE BOTTOM

Butter	⅓ cup (75 ml)
Sugar	1 cup (250 ml)
Honey	¼ cup (50 ml)
Eggs, whole	2
Whipping cream	¼ cup (50 ml)
Pastry flour	1¼ cups (300 ml)
Cocoa	½ cup (125 ml)
Pecan pieces	1 cup (250 ml)

Preheat oven to 350°F (180°C). For brownie bottom, cream butter with sugar and honey. Add eggs, whipping cream, flour and cocoa and mix thoroughly. Stir in pecan pieces.

Butter and flour a 9-inch (23-cm) springform pan and fill with batter. Bake until set. The crust should be soft but not liquid. Cool.

MOUSSE

Belgian chocolate	8 oz (250 g)
Egg whites	3
Granulated sugar	¼ cup (50 ml)
Egg yolks	6
Icing sugar	⅔ cup (150 ml)
Whipped cream	2½ cups (625 ml)
Fresh fruit and more whipped cream	for garnish

Melt chocolate in double boiler. Whip egg whites with granulated sugar until soft peaks form and refrigerate. Whip yolks with icing sugar to the ribbon stage and add melted chocolate. Scrape mixing bowl frequently so chocolate won't harden on the bowl or you'll have chocolate chips in the mousse. Fold whipped cream into mixture, then fold in egg whites.

Spread mousse over cooled brownie bottom and refrigerate or freeze overnight. Unmold and garnish with whipped cream and fresh fruit.

It is not the high cost of living that keeps young people from marriage these days, but the cost of high living; when a young man calls on a young lady now ... he has to take her out—and feed her!

BANFF CRAG AND CANYON, MARCH 29, 1928

Cassatta Ice Cream

Michael Clark, *Executive Chef*
SUNSHINE VILLAGE, BANFF NATIONAL PARK

Serves 8 to 10

Belgian chocolate	6 oz (175 g)
Vanilla ice cream	1¼ quarts (1.25 l)
Frozen raspberries	½ cup (125 ml)
Grenadine	2 – 3 tbsp (30 – 45 ml)
Candied fruit peel	¾ cup (175 ml)

1ST LAYER

Break up chocolate and melt in double boiler. Pour ⅓ of the ice cream into your mixing machine and mix on low speed with the paddle until ice cream is soft. Slowly add melted chocolate while mixing (small chocolate chips will form). Fill 9 x 5 inch (2 l) loaf pan 1 inch (2.5 cm) deep with mixture and put into freezer.

2ND LAYER

When 1st layer has set, repeat using raspberries and grenadine. Return pan to freezer.

3RD LAYER

Repeat using candied fruit peel. Freeze overnight before serving and save any leftover mixture for next time.

TO SERVE

Turn loaf pan upside down and run under warm water, using your hand underneath to catch the cassatta as it falls out. Slice desired number of portions [approximately 1 inch (2.5 cm) thick] and lay on plates. Garnish the plate with fruit slices and whipped cream before serving.

Melissa's Famous Bran Muffins

MELISSA'S RESTAURANT & BAR, BANFF

Makes 12 large muffins

Bran	3 cups (750 ml)
Brown sugar	1¼ cups (300 ml)
Raisins	2 cups (500 ml)
Date pieces	1 cup (250 ml)
Baking powder	1 tbsp (15 ml)
Baking soda	2 tsp (10 ml)
Salt	1 tsp (5 ml)
Cinnamon	2 tbsp (30 ml)
Milk	4 cups (1 l)
Eggs	3
Vegetable oil	⅔ cup (150 ml)
Vanilla extract	1 tsp (5 ml)
Molasses	3 tbsp (45 ml)
Flour	2 cups (500 ml)

Preheat oven to 450°F (230°C). In a large bowl, combine all dry ingredients and date pieces. In another bowl, beat milk, eggs, oil and vanilla extract together at medium speed. Add the dry ingredients to the milk mixture, add molasses and beat for 3 minutes.

Pour the batter into greased chicken pot pie tins (or muffin pans for smaller muffins) and bake for 30 to 40 minutes or until done.

If you don't know why a strawberry short-cake is so called, look for the strawberries.

BANFF CRAG AND CANYON, JUNE 17, 1901

Walnut Gateau

David MacGillivray, *Executive Chef*
JASPER PARK LODGE, JASPER

Makes 1 torte

Unsalted butter	6 tbsp (90 ml)
Icing sugar	¼ cup (50 ml)
Egg yolks	11
Egg whites	11
Granulated sugar	¾ cup (175 ml)
Walnuts, chopped	1⅔ cup (400 ml)
Filberts, ground	⅓ cup (75 ml)
Liqueur *(optional)*	
Ganache (recipe follows)	
More chopped walnuts	for garnish

Preheat oven to 350°F (180°C). Cream together butter and icing sugar very well until creamy. Add egg yolks slowly, creaming continuously until all yolks have been added. *Note:* if mixture looks curdled or split, do not worry.

Whip egg whites and granulated sugar until firm meringue consistency has been reached.

Stir nuts into butter mixture, then carefully fold in the meringue. Pour into a cake ring and bake for approximately 45 minutes.

After cooled, cut cake through middle. Moistening with liqueur (such as Amaretto) is optional. Spread thin layer of ganache on bottom half of torte. Replace top. Cover entire torte thinly with ganache. Place in freezer for approximately ½ hour. Take remaining ganache and pour over torte. Cover sides with some chopped walnuts.

GANACHE　For 1 torte

Whipping cream	1¼ cups (300 ml)
Unsalted butter	1 tsp (5 ml)
Dark chocolate	
(chopped fine)	¾ cup (175 ml)

Bring cream and butter to a boil, then turn off heat. Add chocolate to boiled cream and stir until chocolate has melted.

... the proprietor of the bungalow camp at Storm Mountain, 25 miles from Banff ... never knows how many lunchers the buses will bring her at noon each day ... [so] she has secured carrier pigeons to ... carry messages ... as to the number of guests ..."

THE MORNING ALBERTAN, JULY 15, 1925

Chocolate Paradise

Robert Frost, *Executive Chef*
KILMOREY LODGE, WATERTON

Layers upon layers of chocolate cake separated by a savoury dark chocolate ganache resting on tantalizing sherry sabayon sauce. Garnish with chocolate sauce and fresh seasonal fruit.

Serves 20

Eggs	12
Sugar	1 cup (250 ml)
Salt	pinch
Chocolate	1 lb (500 g)

Preheat oven to 325°F (160°C). Separate the egg yolks from their whites. Combine whites with sugar and whip to make a meringue. Warm yolks and salt in a bain-marie (double boiler). Melt chocolate and add to yolk mix. Fold egg yolk mixture and egg whites together. Spread over 2 greased cookie sheets and bake for approximately 15 minutes.

GANACHE

Cream	3 cups (675 ml)
Chocolate	2½ lb (1.1 kg)

Melt chocolate and add cream. Line a 5 × 10 inch (13 × 25 cm) tupperware dish with Saran wrap. Cut cake into layers to fit in pan. Alternate ganache and cake starting and ending with ganache (6 layers of cake and 7 layers of ganache). Wrap cake in Saran wrap and let set in the refrigerator overnight.

SABAYON SAUCE

Egg yolks	14
Sherry	1½ cups (375 ml)
White wine	⅔ cup (150 ml)
Sugar	1 cup (250 ml)

Combine ingredients in a stainless steel bowl and whisk over hot water bath until thick. Cool in refrigerator.

Presenting the finished dessert: Pour 3 tbsp. (45 ml) of sabayon sauce on a decorative plate. Place a ½-inch (1-cm) slice of Chocolate Paradise on sauce in centre of plate. Pour lines of chocolate sauce over sabayon. Then using a toothpick, draw a decorative pattern of your choice. Garnish with fresh seasonal fruit and serve.

While chatting recently with ... the Banff Crag and Canyon *editor, he remarked: "I can give you a good bear story if you like." "Well, if its spicy enough." "Sure, its about a cinnamon bear."*

BOB EDWARDS' *SUMMER ANNUAL*, 1923

The Banff Springs Hotel, *1920*

The recipes in this book have been perfected specifically for the high altitudes of the Rockies. When preparing some of these dishes at home, some cooking times will have to be adjusted to your elevation. It should also be remembered that different stoves have varying real temperatures (don't totally trust that dial!). The first time you create one of these delicious tastes of the Canadian Rockies, keep a close watch and fine tune the recipe to your kitchen.

The town of Banff sits at an elevation of 4,500 ft (1,400 m), Lake Louise (at the lake) is at 5,500 ft (1,700 m), Canmore is at 4,300 ft (1,310 m), Waterton is at 4,240 ft (1,290 m) and Jasper is at 3,472 ft (1,058 m). The lodges in the back country are at varying elevations. Compared to sea level, at such altitudes water boils at a lower temperature—thus boiling water is actually cooler—and cooking times for processes involving liquids are proportionately longer. A one-minute egg at sea level is a two minute egg in Banff (and a four-minute egg on the almost 10,000 ft/3,000 m summit of nearby Mt. Rundle, should you happen to be up there for breakfast). In general, when cooking at lower elevations, times for Banff recipes involving liquids should be shortened.

The lower air pressures at higher elevations also mean faster evaporation. Foods cooked in Banff will lose moisture more rapidly that those cooked at sea level; as such, less liquids are required for preparing Banff recipes at lower elevations. As a guideline, decrease liquids by 2 to 3 tablespoons (30 to 45 ml) for each cup (250 ml) called for when preparing a Banff recipe at sea level.

Still another effect of lower air pressures is that the gases in baked goods will expand more rapidly than at sea level. To compensate, when preparing Banff baking recipes at sea level, increase baking soda or powder by about ¼ teaspoon (1 ml) for each teaspoon (5 ml) required, increase sugar by about 2 to 3 tablespoons (30 to 45 ml) for each cup (250 ml) called for, beat eggs vigorously, and decrease oven temperatures by about 25°F (15°C). And don't forget to adjust the liquids as well; a moist cake recipe in Banff can become a mush cake recipe at sea level!

A little experimentation will usually be required to create perfect results in your home kitchen. But then, besides the eating, that's the fun part of cooking anyway.

Credits

The colour photographs throughout the book are courtesy of the renowned photographer, Douglas Leighton. A dramatic collection of his work can be found in his bestselling book, *The Canadian Rockies* (Rocky Mountain Books). Translated into several languages it makes a great memory to compliment this book!

All historic photographs are from the collection of the Whyte Museum of the Canadian Rockies, Banff, Alberta and are used with their permission.

Edwards, Bob, *Summer Annuals*, 1921, 1923, 1924

Dempsey, Hugh A., *Indian Names for Alberta Communities*, (Calgary: Glenbow Museum, 1987)

Jessup, Elon, *Camp Grub*, (New York: E.P. Dutton and Company, 1924)

Leighton, Douglas, *A Taste of Banff*, (Banff: A Taste of Publishing, 1985)

MacGregor, James G., *Pack Saddles to Tête Jaune Cache* (McClelland and Stewart Limited, 1962)

Robinson, Bart, *Banff Springs: The Story of a Hotel*, (Banff: Summerthought, Limited, 1973)

Roper, Edward, *By Track and Trail: A Journey Through Canada* (London: W.H. Allen & Co., 1891)

Schaffer, Mary T.S., *Old Indian Trails of the Canadian Rockies* (New York: The Knickerbocker Press, 1911)

Sladen, Douglas, *On the Cars and Off* (London: Ward, Lock and Bowden Limited, 1895)

Williams, M.B., *Jasper National Park* (Department of the Interior, 1928)

"Report of the Rocky Mountain Parks of Canada" by Howard Douglas, Superintendent (for the years 1903, 1906 and 1911)

"Report of the Commissioner of Dominion Parks" by Howard Douglas, 1911

"Report of Jasper Park" by R.S. Stronach, acting Superintendent (yearly report for 1918–1919)

Crag and Canyon, Banff, 1901–1931

Calgary Herald, 1886

The Morning Albertan, Calgary, 1912, 1925

Canadian Alpine Journal, Vol. II, No. 1 (Alpine Club of Canada, 1909)

Contributors and their recipes (page numbers in brackets)

BAKER CREEK BISTRO Banff National Park: Broiled Shrimp with an Asian Sauce (20); Scallop Salad with Balsamic Vinaigrette (42); Broiled Chicken Breast with a Strawberry Cantaloupe Salsa (81); Banana Rum Crêpes (130).

BALKAN The Greek Restaurant, Banff: Delicious Cheese Rolls (Tiropeta) (15); Hearty Moussaka (74); Special Galatoboureko (129).

BANFF PARK LODGE Banff: Shanghai Shrimp (24); Coconut Curry Chicken (86); Carrot Cake (134).

BANFF SPRINGS HOTEL; Grilled Belgian Endive Salad with Sea Scallops and Roasted Tomato and Garlic Dressing (52); Banff: Carrot Ginger Soup with Mussels and Scallops (54); Chicken Breast with Orange Coriander Sauce (98).

BUFFALO MOUNTAIN LODGE Banff: Buffalo Satay (14); Parsnip, Honey and Lime Soup (39); Apple-Marinated Cornish Game Hen (73); Bumbleberry Pie (126).

BUMPER'S BEEF HOUSE RESTAURANT Banff: Bumper's Beef Barley Soup (41); Canadian Mountain Stew (78).

CANADIAN MOUNTAIN HOLIDAYS Bugaboo Lodge, BC: Curry-Glazed Pork Chops (80).

CHATEAU JASPER Jasper: Tarragon Salad Julienne (34); Chicken Almondine au Curry (106); Caramel Hazelnut Pear Crumble (122); Chocolate Apricot Hazelnut Torte (124).

CHATEAU LAKE LOUISE Lake Louise: Beef Stroganoff (109); Pear William Fondue (117); Strawberries Romanoff (118).

COYOTE'S DELI AND GRILL Banff: Cilantro Chili Mayonnaise (16); Green Chili Cilantro Vinaigrette (40); Killer Pancakes (114).

DEER LODGE Lake Louise: Spinach and Cambozola Cheese Wrapped in Phyllo with Fresh Fruit Salsa (8).

EMERALD LAKE LODGE Yoho National Park: Baked Goat Cheese Wrapped in Phyllo Pastry (18); Caribou Loin with Peppercorn Crust (76).

FIDDLE RIVER SEAFOOD COMPANY Jasper: Hot Artichoke, Cheddar and Crab Dip (13).

GRIZZLY HOUSE Banff: Grizzly House Salad (44); Hunter Fondue (82).

GUIDO'S RISTORANTE Banff: Basil Sauce—Pesto (63); Sweet Cheese Custard (116).

INNS OF BANFF PARK Banff: Smoked Trout Crostini (10); Quesadilla with Hot Italian Sausage and Avocado Salsa (12); Exotic Greens and Prosciutto with Lemon Goat Cheese Dressing (38); Chicken Breast with Goat Cheese and Sun-dried Tomato Salsa (68); Fettucine with Tomato Basil Cream (72); Royal Kir Granita (118).

JASPER PARK LODGE Jasper: Northern Mushroom Soup (55); Buttermilk Baking Powder Biscuits (56); Herb Roasted Chicken (108); Walnut Gateau (144).

JOSHUA'S RESTAURANT Banff: Baked Camembert (22); Mussels with Saffron Sauce (23); Mixed Salad with Tarragon Dressing (43); Chocolate Mousse Cake (132).

KILMOREY LODGE Waterton: Okonoki Salad (59); Elk Kilmorey with Saskatoon Sauce (102); Chocolate Paradise (146).

LAKE O'HARA LODGE Yoho National Park: Garlic Herb Soufflé (11); Raspberry and Balsamic Vinaigrette (33); Spiced Butternut Squash Soup (35); Chilled Fruit Soups (Melon Soup, Berry Soup) (36); Fresh Salmon Spiral with Sun-dried Tomato Herb Butter (62); Baked Chicken Breast with Fresh Basil and Roasted Garlic (64); Swiss Potatoes (65); Pear Tarte Tatin (119); Chocolate Pecan Tarte (120).

LAKE LOUISE STATION RESTAURANT Lake Louise: Poppy Seed Lemon Yogurt Dressing (32); Salmon-Stuffed Chicken Breast (70).

LE BEAUJOLAIS Banff: Cold Corn Soup with Smoked Salmon (58); Crème Brûlée (136).

LODGE AT KANANASKIS/HOTEL KANANASKIS Kananaskis: Veal Tortellini with Shrimp Cream Herb Sauce (27); Tiger Prawns (28); Char-Grilled Beef Tenderloin (96); Chocolate Decadent Cake (140).

MAGPIE & STUMP RESTAURANT AND CANTINA Banff: Queso Sopas (Cheese Soup) (46).

MELISSA'S RESTAURANT & BAR Banff: Melissa's Chicken (104); Melissa's Famous Bran Muffins (143).

MOUNT ASSINIBOINE LODGE Mount Assiniboine Provincial Park: Fruit and Buttermilk Pancakes (137); Smoked Gruyère Cheese Salad (48); Eggplant Parmigiana (88); Baked Salmon Fillet with Sesame Caper Butter (105); Sunburst Plum Cake (135).

MOUNT ENGADINE LODGE Kananaskis: Raspberry Vinaigrette (51); Chicken Breast with Tarragon-Yogurt Sauce (95); Apple Strudel "Mount Engadine" (128).

MOUNT ROYAL HOTEL Banff: Fresh Scallops with Beet and Red Cabbage Sauce (26); Mushroom Ragout on Four Colours (29); Belgian Endive and Oak Leaf Salad with Pumpkin Dressing (50); Lamb Loin with Pear William Sauce and Garlic (92); Beef and Veal Tender-loin with Madeira Sauce (94); Fresh Fruit and Berry Timbale with Grand Marnier Ice Cream (138).

PAPA GEORGE'S Jasper: Vegetarian Burrito (25); Vegetarian Chili (101).

PEPPERMILL RESTAURANT Canmore: Creme de Veau Chasseur (45); Pork Tenderloin Dijonnaise (85); Berries Gratin (133).

RIMROCK RESORT HOTEL Banff: Winter Squash Soup with Scallops (47); Fillet of Sea Bass with fresh Mediterranean Herbs and Red Pepper Sauce (91).

SHERWOOD HOUSE Canmore: Vegetable Korma (66).

SKOKI LODGE Banff National Park: Skoki Health Bread (17); Stuffed Salmon (77); Poppyseed Cake (112); Clafouti (115).

SUNSHINE VILLAGE SKI & SUMMER RESORT Banff National Park: Salad Eagle's Nest (57); Veal Francesca (97); Fillet of Salmon Natasha (100); Cassatta Ice Cream (142).

TICINO RESTAURANT Banff: Ticino Marinated Salmon (19); Chicken Breast Ticino (84); Gelato al Caffe Ticino (127).

Index